My Heart's Journey

Chasing Love through Europe on a Motor Scooter
A Memoir

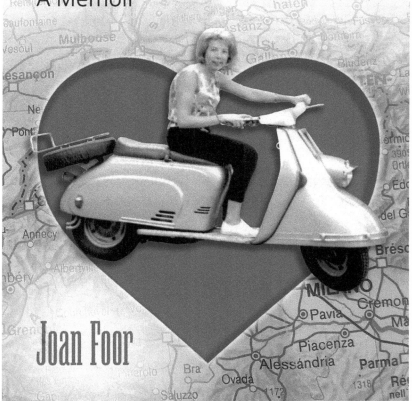

Joan Foor

ISBN 978-1-7324567-9-2 (paperback)
Library of Congress Control Number: 2020915151

Published by Foor Publishing
Cathedral City, California

Author: Joan Foor

Editor: Lynn Jones Green

Cover Map: Used with permission from
East View Map Link www.evmaplink.com/

Cover/interior design and layout:
Mark E. Anderson, www.aquazebra.com

Printed in the United States of America

Acknowledgments

The journey reflected in this book would not have occurred without having met Paco Hidalgo. Meeting his wonderful family in Spain was one of the highlights of my life.

I want to thank the late Serge Dodillon, of Paris, France who shared his city with me. We met again years later and continued to keep in touch for decades via telephone.

Val Brooks Ciccone who I met in Weisbaden, Germany and I became lifelong friends. Her recent passing was a loss for me and her family.

Thanks to Fran Babb who was responsible for extending my trip via her 1956 Opal farther throughout Europe and Scandinavia. She fulfilled her promise to her mother and aunt from Brooklyn, New York.

Pam Ahlgrim, RD., my closest friend, has listened to my account of these experiences over the years repetitively. Her never ending encouragement helped me to bring this memoir to life.

My cousins: Debbie Darnell, Karyn Espenlaub and Linda Raneri who reside in Pennsylvania have supported my story telling and writing for years. Cousin, Donna Carson, has kept safe the original newspaper clipping of my journey sharing it first with her daughters and now granddaughters. She commented several times recently, "Hurry and get that book finished before my eyesight fails and I'm unable to read it!"

Former co-workers and great friends: Mary Jo Boley, Helen Liebal and Joyce Orner met with me right before and after my journey and we have continued to get together for decades. Their support and encouragement to write about this trip have help spur me forward.

Fellow authors and the best of friends Grace Robbins, author of *Cinderella and the Carpetbagger* and Cynda Thomas, author of *He Came from the Sky; Hell of a Ride; The wasp and the Hornet;* and the *Cowboy's Alien Abduction* have shared with me their experiences as writers. Their unwavering support in this project helped me to continue on to the finish.

Dedication

Dedicated to
My beloved mother, father and brother

My Heart's Journey

Chasing Love through Europe on a Motor Scooter

A memoir by Joan L. Foor, MN, RN

Table of Contents

Prologue

There is something about a pandemic that causes a person to contemplate the past, present and future of their life. At least, that was my experience in the spring of 2020. Sitting alone I had many hours to recall the events that had led me to where I am today—a former Nurse Practitioner and retired Army Lieutenant Colonel enjoying later life in Palm Springs, California. I have made it my life's mission to help and support people. The isolation imposed by COVID-19 has been surreal and unnatural, especially for someone like me who thrives on being with people. I gain much pleasure supporting my friends and family with advice—welcome and unwelcome—and sharing my life stories where I think it might help or elevate their mood.

I have always been a storyteller drawing from my experiences in childhood in rural Pennsylvania or from managing a fraught upbringing with an erratic mother and broken father. But some of my favorite stories come from my travels throughout Europe in 1964. I was twenty-eight, overconfident and naïve. Driven by my lust for travel and an (insistent) boyfriend, I took off for Europe eager to see the wonders of the world but without much of a plan. I've shared true stories of what took place with friends and relatives. I know now it was the trip of my lifetime. In all my worldwide travel since, I have never felt as free and unafraid. This I now view in such a stark contrast to the present environment of pandemic.

While clearing my closet I stumbled upon my actual diary and memorabilia from my first trip throughout Europe. It was so comforting to relive the experience through those twenty-eight-year-old eyes and heart. I decided to use the time spent at home these past few months to extract from my diary the true account of more experiences and adventures traveling as a solo female. My travels through thousands of miles alone on the open road (via a German motor scooter) may have been one of the wonders of the world at that time. I never ran into another woman out on the open road—let alone, on a motor scooter. I was so unaware and innocent, I now fear for my younger self.

My desire is that this memoir will serve to document a point in time in Europe in 1964. A trip such as this was unusual then and, undoubtedly, even more unusual now. I doubt it could even be possible today. I hope you enjoy reliving this adventure with me.

—Joan L. Foor

Chapter One: Aboard Air France

On July 12, 1964, at 6:55 a.m., I arrived at Paris Orly Airport. What a flight! It had been an adventurous night aboard Air France.

Once airborne, I got situated in my economy aisle seat. The window seat next to me wasn't taken. I looked forward to being able to spread out and get comfortable during the night. Shortly after getting settled, I was welcomed by a young handsome gentleman across the aisle.

"Hello. I'm Paulo, from Persia. Where are you headed?" he asked.

I was hesitant to answer but responded rather abruptly, "Well, for now, Paris." I didn't want to start a conversation. My attention went to thumbing through my French dictionary. I began to practice French pronunciations from common English words when I was interrupted again.

"Where are you from?" Paulo inquired.

"Currently from Los Angeles but originally from Pennsylvania."

At this point, I realized it was going to be difficult to discourage a dialogue with this man; I could simply be rude and tell Paulo outright I didn't want to talk with him. As I was deciding upon the words to excuse myself gracefully, my thoughts were interrupted with, "This is your captain speaking. I am unable to warm the cabin. It will be a very cold flight. The stewardesses will be passing out blankets."

I accepted the two packages of blankets provided by the stewardess as she went down the aisle. I laid them on the seat beside me. It didn't take long before I was tearing the plastic from my small blankets and draping them over my shoulders. Cold air was circulating from above and I began to shiver. I placed my hands up to my mouth and tried blowing warm air into my hands to keep them warm.

"It's going to be a long miserable flight. I'm headed to Persia to visit the tomb of my grandmother," Paulo offered.

"I'm sorry to hear that," I said.

"Thank you; it is sad. However, the good part is to be able to visit with my family. I've been away for a few years," he remarked.

Paulo had bronze skin; his face was well shaven, and his charcoal black hair was combed neatly straight back from his forehead. He wore a white, tailored, silk shirt tucked neatly into pin-striped light-gray slacks and expensive-looking, well-shined shoes.

We continued to share small talk across the aisle for about an hour. The plane was miserably cold. I couldn't get comfortable.

"Move over here," Paulo said, patting the cushion of the seat beside him. "It will be easier to talk and keep warm."

I paused, realizing that he was a complete stranger. However, through our conversations, I began to sense that he was trustworthy and not flirtatious. My feet were frigid, and every few minutes I was rubbing the calves of my legs to increase circulation. My lips were quivering and my teeth began to chatter spontaneously.

"Come," he continued. "I can see you are shivering."

I hadn't been this cold in a long time and felt frozen. Reluctantly, I gathered my blankets, and purse and moved across the aisle. Paulo removed his shoes, helped me slip out of my spiked high heels and wrapped blankets around both of our feet and lower legs together. I felt almost an immediate warm relief once his legs were hugging mine. Sheer nylon stockings and a tailored, two-piece linen suit were of no help to keep me warm across the aisle. He pushed the armrest out of our way. I helped spread out the blankets to cover my chest and overlapped to his. Together we stretched out other small blankets across both our mid-sections and laps. It didn't take too long before both of us stopped shivering. Here I was wrapped together with a stranger, but it was essential to keep warm.

I shared with Paulo stories of my happy childhood along the Juniata River, which carved its way through Southern Pennsylvania. Tales of how my brother and I fished, swam and explored that river while growing up. Also, how things had gone so wrong in my early twenties when my father became an alcoholic and was no longer faithful to my mother. Making matters worse, his mistress turned out to be our former housekeeper. It was for that reason I left my beautiful home state and moved to California.

Paulo and I continued to share our experiences through the night. I saw the stewardess take a second glance our way each time she walked down the aisle. I suspect she wondered if there was something going on under those blankets. (There wasn't.) Paulo was a perfect gentleman.

I was fascinated hearing about Paulo's childhood and life in Persia. He explained how he had adjusted to the American way of life and that he would remain in America. Paulo showed an interest in my plans to marry Paco, who had been a soccer player. I talked about how we met on the tennis court and it was almost love at first sight. Still single at twenty-eight, I believed I had finally met the man of my dreams. I shared with Paulo my excitement about going to meet my future mother-in-law and Paco's family in Barcelona. I mentioned how I had longed for years to see Paris. This would be my opportunity to see not only "Paree" but hopefully as much of Europe as possible along the way.

We were two strangers from two different worlds headed in different directions. Paulo would travel on to Persia; I would vacation a few days in Paris and then head for Barcelona.

"Prepare for landing," the stewardess announced. "Bring your seats to the upright position and restore your tray tables. We will be landing shortly." Paulo helped me unwrap the blankets. I slipped into my shoes and reached for my purse. Holding onto my blankets I stood up and turned toward Paulo.

"It was nice meeting you. I really enjoyed our time together." I extended my hand in gratitude, he reciprocated and helped me get steady on my feet. We returned smiles.

"Lots of luck with your plans, Joan. It's been fun getting to know you," he said.

"And the same to you, Paulo," I replied.

Once across the aisle, I scooted over to the window seat. My heart began to beat faster when I saw the lights of Paris below. I thought, *This could have been a miserable, long, cold flight, but thanks to Paulo it was made shorter and more comfortable.*

As the plane circled for landing, I was glued to the window. The skyline with the lights on the monuments and tall buildings were lit up like a gold Christmas trees. Some lights appeared as if they were blinking on and off.

My desire to see Paree had been on a steady increase. My brother, Les, recently returned home from Europe. He had been stationed with the U.S. Air Force in Madrid and North Africa. He shared pictures of Paris and other places he'd visited. Les aroused my curiosity further, not only about Paris, but Tangiers, Casa Blanca, Madrid and many other interesting places. Thoughts ran through my mind as we circled the airport in a holding pattern.

When I was twelve, my brother fourteen, our Mother had taken us by train from Pennsylvania to Los Angeles. She said, "This trip is to educate you both. I want to show you there is more to the United States than what exists here in our small town of Altoona, Pennsylvania." We stopped for three weeks in Roswell, New Mexico. Our uncle took us to Santa Fe, Carlsbad Caverns and other sites in New Mexico.

We continued by train to Los Angeles and stayed with my great aunt Anna. Some of the places I remember were Hollywood, Pacific Ocean Park, Sea World, Knott's Berry Farm and Dodger Stadium.

My great-aunt Anna told me about how my great-uncle Will, Aunt Anna's brother, moved to Los Angeles from Pennsylvania around 1912. He went home to Altoona to visit, and Aunt Anna was fascinated by the way he dressed. He wore colorful shirts, white slacks and white shoes. Aunt Anna heard from him how desirable the climate was, about the Red Line train everyone road to downtown, the tall palm trees and the Pacific Ocean. When she turned twenty, she left home and traveled to meet her brother in California. When I was young all the relatives spoke about Aunt Anna being the black sheep of the family. According to Mother it was simply because in those days single young ladies did not leave home nor travel alone. For her to go to California really shocked her family.

Aunt Anna told me she only attended school to the eighth grade. She had studied on her own to become a real estate broker. Aunt Anna had built three houses and was doing well. I wanted to show her my gratitude for her showing me all around Los Angeles. She had two large yards, one in back and one around the house she owned next door. She mentioned their needing to be cut.

After she went to work, I used her lawnmower and spent several hours grooming her lawns. That evening I developed a high fever and was delirious. Mother and Aunt Anna used cooling measures through the night to get my fever down. They telephoned a doctor who came to the house early the next morning. He suspected I had developed polio, because my legs were stiff and I was feverish and confused. Aunt Anna blamed herself for mentioning the lawns needed cut. The doctor prescribed medication and told mother to continue with cold cloths as long as I had a fever.

"If her fever breaks and she can move her extremities in two days, you don't need to call me back. Otherwise, if little Joan worsens, or if there is no improvement, then I need to see her," he said.

Two days later I was feeling better. Mother and Aunt Anna were so relieved. Aunt Anna thanked me for doing the lawns but made me promise to stay out of the sun during the day unless she or mother were with me. When we were ready to leave L.A. and were waiting on our train, I remember Aunt Anna's last words to my brother at the Alameda Train Station: "Leslie, now that you have visited Los Angeles, where would you prefer to live—here or in Altoona, Pennsylvania?"

"I'm not sure, Aunt Anna. But I think in Altoona," he answered.

"Well, just remember this: If someone were to ask you where

you are from and you say Altoona, they will say, 'Where?' But if your answer is Los Angeles, everyone knows where that is!"

If she had asked me the same question I would have answered differently. I loved California and would prefer Los Angeles. It was the brightness of the sun every day. There were so many gray and rainy days in Pennsylvania. All the houses in L.A. looked more modern and as though they were freshly painted.

The beautiful Pacific Ocean was so vast and inviting. On our visit, Mother had said I could take off my shoes, but I was not to get my good dress wet.

"Go out a little farther," Les urged.

I was wary of the waves washing onto shore. Les yelled, "You are a disgrace and afraid of your own shadow." He was daring me to venture out farther.

I walked farther out from shore. A large wave came in and slapped against my chest. My good dress was soaked. Aunt Anna had to wrap a blanket around me. That ended the day at the beach. Mother was furious with me—but it was my brother's fault.

Mother surprised Les and me with an extended trip to Mexico City after L.A. It turned out to be a challenge. Visiting a foreign country where a different language was spoken was an eye opener. Men were wearing large sombreros, riding on fine horses. Their saddles were laden with genuine silver. They proudly rode their horses up and down the wide boulevards in the historic center. It made me want to ride a horse too.

Mother rented horses for us to go riding in Chapultepec Park. She said, "This is one of the largest parks in the western hemisphere." That didn't mean much to us except the park was huge.

We picked out horses with worn, leather saddles, which were a far cry from those we had seen with all the silver. Les and I did take notice of all the vendors in the park selling leather belts, wallets and hand-crafted silver.

Mother arranged a tour through a silver, pottery and glass-blowing factory during our two weeks in Mexico City. We learned a lot and had loads of fun. I would probably have to thank Mother—or blame her—for this desire to travel and my adventurous spirit.

This trip to Europe would be a long-awaited adventure. It wouldn't be like my annual two-week vacations for the past ten years. The trips I remember most while working as a long-distance telephone switchboard operator in Pennsylvania were going to Atlantic City or Wildwood, New Jersey. Once when Les was on leave, we visited New York City; and one winter, I vacationed in Miami, Florida.

Since transferring to Pacific Telephone in Los Angeles, I hadn't accrued vacation time until now. My position now was as a service representative at the Hollywood Business Office. I was required to sell princess telephones, bell chimes, and additional telephone extensions for the home or office. It was a high-pressure job. We had a quota of how many additional phones and chimes we were expected to sell. When customers telephoned about their bills, we only had twenty seconds to run to a central location, find their records, and get back on the telephone. After addressing the subscribers' questions, we went straight into the sales pitch. Supervisors monitored our calls. We never knew when they were listening in. Regardless of customers' verbal objections, we had to high-pressure them into buying additional phones or fancier ones. I was a nervous wreck trying to meet the company's expectations.

One of my best friends, Jan, who worked at the same job, had resigned and moved to Northern Norway to live with her aunts on a farm. I missed her and wished I could escape too. My vacation time was approaching and if ever there were a time to get away from here, this was it!

I requested a six-month leave of absence to get away from the job and to travel to Spain specifically. I was surprised when it was granted. For the first time since graduating from high school, I'd be free for more than two weeks. I had saved enough money to last for months.

The question remained, how was I going to explain to my boyfriend, Paco, why I needed to vacation now *and* without him? I had several main reasons. First, I wanted to eliminate the pressure from my job. Secondly, Paco, the love of my life, was pressuring me to move in with him. I was drawn to him like a magnet and had lost control of my convictions. He didn't understand why, when two people are in love, they would have to marry to live together. I tried to explain my religious upbringing. He was romantic, a great dancer and a tough challenge for me. And I don't mean just on the tennis court. Girlfriends of mine were jealous of our relationship. They flirted and paraded around trying to get his attention. Paco ignored their silly advances. I had his undivided attention, no matter where we went or what we were doing.

I was torn between my religion upbringing and my passion for this man. Was my love for him strong enough to leave my home and move to Barcelona? For now, to leave my country and family behind seemed impossible. These were questions needing answers. I hoped that after traveling to Spain no questions would remain. I had to promise Paco I would visit and stay with his mother in Barcelona until he arrived sometime later. I did share with him about visiting my friend Jan who had recently moved from Norway to Wiesbaden, Germany. Plans I didn't discuss with him were to see as much of Europe on my way as possible.

As I suspected, Paco just didn't see or understand the urgency of my trip.

"We can travel together one of these days. Why do you have to go now?" he asked. Paco continued to look puzzled during our last evening and conversation together.

"Joan, you should not travel to Europe or to Barcelona alone," Paco said. "It is not safe," he added. I promised to stay with his mother in Spain to get him to calm down.

"My job is killing me," I replied. "You don't realize how hard it is. I need a break before I have a heart attack or nervous breakdown. I've accrued vacation time, which must be taken now, or I'll lose some of it."

"Joan, you aren't going to have a heart problem," Paco said jokingly. "Come live with me. Forget about the job. Quit!"

He didn't realize he had become part of my problem; I needed some breathing space.

Being from Spain, Paco Hidalgo, after all my explanations, still didn't understand my reluctance to move in with him. I could no longer follow my religious guidelines when he was near. Paco was a handsome, well-built thirty-six-year-old who had recently retired as a professional soccer player from Barcelona. He retired at the top of his career and moved to Los Angeles. Paco's wavy, brown, sun-bleached hair, pearly white teeth, and manly body on the tennis court attracted my attention. Once I was introduced, I began to fall in love with him. His broken English accent and foreign mannerisms were an added attraction. A close friend asked me how I knew his love for me was true love. I shared with her the following experience:

> One day I twisted my ankle on the tennis court. Paco jumped over the tennis net, quickly removed my shoe and sweaty sock. Chills went up and down my spine as he gently examined my foot and ankle. He rubbed my foot and lower leg, and then he kissed my sweaty foot in different places ever so gently. Paco carried me to his car, drove me home, and helped me into the house to the couch to rest.

I believe it was then that I fell madly in love with Paco. I had never had any man in my life show such tenderness and compassion toward me. When I spoke, he looked into my eyes and gave me his undivided attention. I had enjoyed a lot of male companionships over the years and was close to marriage several times, but no man had ever shown such a sincere interest in me and everything about me.

However, Paco did have a quick temper. He complained about the food in restaurants, especially the produce. It was never fresh enough. Paco would frown, remarking, "No fresco." I was embarrassed at times for the waitress or waiter. He bragged about his own garden vegetables and raising chickens outside of Barcelona. I did agree with him that the air by the ocean in Spain had to be better than smoggy Los Angeles. There were days in L.A. we were warned not to play tennis due to the smog hovering over Los Feliz Boulevard.

His temperament did weigh into my decision. A trip to visit Paco's family would give me a better understanding of his behaviors. Also, this was an opportunity to learn more about Spain and their customs. However, questions remained. Was I blinded by passion, his good looks and foreign accent? And would absence make my love grow even stronger?

Chapter Two: Paris

It was breaking dawn by the time I checked my bags at a place adjacent to the airport and boarded a bus marked "Paris." My brother gave me a few francs before I left. I handed these lightweight coins to the bus driver. He rattled off in French and by the raised tone of his voice and glare there was something wrong with the coins. Not understanding, I held out some new silver francs I just exchanged for a twenty-dollar bill at the airport. He grabbed a couple of francs and gave me some weird looking light weight coins as change. Apparently, the Francs my brother gave me were no longer good. When the bus approached what appeared to me to be the outskirts of Paris, I got off. I couldn't wait to put my feet on the streets of Paris. This is where I'd longed to be for years. I stepped down onto the cobblestone street, almost stumbling in my beige spike heeled shoes, matching purse and burnt orange tailored made linen silk lined suit.

I was so excited. It was like having a deep, wonderful dream. I looked in every direction, taking it all in like a wide-angled camera. After about the distance of a city block, I was approached by a young man on a motorbike. He came up alongside of me. There was a saddle bag across the back wheel of his bike, full of folded newspapers. He jumped from his motorbike, turned off the engine and began to tag alongside of me. The French dictionary I was studying in the plane, I inadvertently checked in with my baggage by mistake. Very few French words remained as part of my vocabulary. In English, I said, "I need to get near the Opera House." He smiled, spoke more French and pointed a finger motioning like it was straight ahead in the distance. I shook my head and said, "*Je ne comprends pas*" ("I don't understand")—one phrase I remembered. And I repeated, "I want to go to the Opera House." A friend who had been to Paris recently told me the Opera House was a good central location to look for a hotel.

"*Venez ici,*" he said. He appeared excited, pointing to the cement steps leading down to the river. A mist, like the lifting of a fog, was rising from the water. I thought, *This must be the Seine River.* He propped his cycle against the overpass wall and pulled at my arm. His eyes were sparkling with excitement as they met mine. He had a huge smile from ear to ear. It was apparent there was something for me to see down by the river's edge. It wasn't easy in spiked high heels, hurrying with him pulling at my arm down wide cement steps to under the overpass.

Suddenly he slid his arm around my waist, pulled me close and tried to kiss me. I was shocked! I kept turning my face away from his lips and said, "No, No, *tout de suite*, Opera House!" This was so crazy. He was determined but I managed to push him back saying, "*Tout de suite!*"

He looked puzzled. It took only seconds to find there wasn't anything for me to see by the river except his flirtations. Realizing I wasn't going to be kissing him along the Seine at daybreak, he let go of me. I turned quickly and rushed back up the stairs. He followed close behind and began speaking in French what sounded to me to be rather apologetic.

I started walking more quickly back toward the bus line in disgust, not looking over my shoulder. Suddenly, he appeared by my side pushing his motorbike. I believe he was trying to tell me he would help me after all. A taxi went by and he flagged it down. After fastening his cycle to a light post, he spoke rapidly in French to the driver. Luckily for both of us the cab driver spoke English. "He wants to help pick up your baggage and will take you to a nice hotel by the Opera House, *tres bien?*" I was relieved to know he intended to direct me to a hotel.

"Yes, that's fine. I appreciate it," I said to our translating driver.

"Je m'appelle Luke," came from the back seat.

The cab driver said, "He goes by the name, Luke."

"Thank you, merci," I said, surprising myself by remembering the word for "thank you" after such a strange encounter by the Seine River. Luke smiled with a devilish-looking grin and nodded his head when his name was mentioned.

I handed the baggage card with the address to the cab driver. When we arrived at the baggage claim, Luke went with me as I presented the claim ticket. He picked up my two light-blue Lady Baltimore bags, and I carried my cosmetic case. We rejoined our cab driver waiting at the curb. Luke and the cab driver exchanged conversations in French as I enjoyed the ride through the Paris city streets. The driver drove almost a full circle around the Opera House and turned down a very narrow street marked Rue Godot-de-Mauroy. He parked in front of a sign that read "Hotel des Capucines."

A bellman from the hotel approached the cab. Luke spoke in French and the bellman helped Luke carry my bags into the hotel.

I paid the taxi driver and entered the small quaint lobby. It was like entering a French foreign-film set. The elevator was small with a black expandable wire door. The Frenchman behind the counter spoke English advising it would be twenty-seven francs per day. I signed the register and the bellman stacked my luggage against the back of the elevator. He and I could barely squeeze in front of the luggage as he pulled the wire elevator door shut. It was a jerky stop after passing several floors. I followed the bellman down a dark hallway and noticed a W.C. sign above one of the doors ahead. I wondered what "W.C." stood for when the bellman said, "Mademoiselle, the toilette is there." He spoke good English. My question was answered; that was my bathroom.

He opened the door to my room. It was clean, quaint, with large pink-flowered patterned wallpaper. There were two windows side by side at the far corner of the room. There was a tiny sink against the wall on my right next to what looked like a toilet low to the floor. I was checking out the room while he went back to the elevator for my other suitcase. I wasn't sure how much to tip him as he placed a large bronze metal key on my dresser. I held out several new francs in the palm of my hand. He took two and said, "Merci." As soon as he closed the door behind him, I flopped down on the bed to see how firm the mattress was. It was a bit lumpy.

Suddenly, there was a knock on the door. I opened the door part-way with reluctance. What a surprise to see Luke standing there with a big, happy grin. He had turned out to be of help with my baggage and getting me to this hotel. I let him step into the doorway He spoke in French, pointing to the 5 on his watch. "Oui, oui, *aperitif.*" I gathered from his pointing to his watch he wanted to meet me at five o'clock for a cocktail.

Trying hard to understand and being off-guard, Luke gently pushed me off balance onto the bed. He tried kissing me again and again. I kept resisting, turning my head from side to side. I repeated, "No, no!"

Provoked, I used all my strength and forcefully pushed him away. I stood up, "Luke, that's enough!" I opened the door and motioned for him to get out. He finally realized I meant my "No."

He started to leave, turned around with a squeamish look and pointed back to his watch saying, *"Au revoir."*

I thought, *This guy doesn't give up.* He was about an inch taller than me, fair-skinned, not at all attractive with his medium brown, uncombed hair. I should have known what to expect. I had heard stories about the Frenchmen and their advances. I half-smiled at my being so naïve. I knew now. I had arrived.

I unpacked my large suitcase and placed my wrinkled skirts and blouses on hangers. I looked out the window and watched the people pass by. I was tired but could not get enough of the scene below. Finally, I lay across the bed and dosed off. My sleep was interrupted by a knock on the door. I opened the door cautiously.

"Mademoiselle, a gentleman is asking for you at the desk," said the bellboy.

I looked at my watch; it was five o'clock. I replied to the young man, "Please tell him I'll be a few minutes. Thank you."

I freshened my makeup, brushed my teeth, combed my hair, and quickly slipped into a skirt and blouse outfit that wasn't badly wrinkled. I went down the hall to the W.C. before pushing the button for the elevator. The same bellman opened the wire elevator door and accompanied me down to the lobby. Luke was standing there with a big flirtatious grin. His hair was combed neatly straight back. His light-yellow shirt was neatly tucked into beige trousers with creases. A taller, lean gentleman with black, thinning hair, a pleasant French-looking nose, and dark eyes was standing in the background. He was dressed in a single-breasted tweed sport coat and gabardine slacks. The bellman and Luke smiled and nodded to one another.

"*Enchanté* . . . excuse my English," spoke Luke's taller friend. He stepped forward to greet me. I extended my right hand. He accepted and leaned forward, kissing me gently on both cheeks. I reared backward rather startled.

He looked at me directly and explained, "I'm Luke's friend, Serge. He asked me to join the two of you this evening to translate for him. I don't know English well; I mean, I'll try." Luke and Serge exchanged some words in French. I did recognize the word "Bonjour" as they both nodded to the bellman. Luke hurried ahead and opened the door for us. Serge followed me outside and I walked between the two men down the narrow sidewalk.

"Luke told me how you met. He wanted me to join you both for an aperitif," Serge remarked.

"I must admit I didn't understand Luke earlier," I said. "When he pointed to the 5 on his watch, I gathered he was going to return." My thoughts were, *I didn't approve of his aggressive advances toward me earlier. And I wonder what an aperitif is.*

We walked a few blocks with Serge and Luke exchanging comments in French. Serge said to me, "Luke wants to know if your hotel is comfortable."

"Tell him that I like it and I appreciate his escorting me there," I said, and I looked over at Luke and smiled as I spoke. Serge repeated my answer in French.

Luke spoke to Serge, and Serge looked at me and said, "He

asked, where in the United States do you come from?"

I answered, "I live in California now, but I was born in Pennsylvania."

Serge pointed to a sidewalk café and led us to an outside table. Luke positioned a chair for me to sit beside him and gave me a flirtatious glance. Serge motioned for the waiter. The round table was so small, our knees were touching underneath. Luke pointed to the menu in the center.

"I'll have a glass of wine," I said. Serge ordered three Martini's. When I heard 'Martini' I thought I would have to sip it real slow. I was fascinated hearing the French words coming from nearby tables and people edging around us. It was very congested. We raised our glasses and, to my surprise, after a small sip I realized it wasn't a martini like the ones we drink in America. It tasted like a sweet red wine with a squeezed lemon rind dangling on the edge of the glass.

Luke spoke in French to Serge. Serge related, "Luke wants to know what brings you to Paris?"

I looked straight at Luke, "Well, I'm on my way to meet my future mother-in-law in Barcelona."

Serge repeated in French what I said. Luke leaned forward with a puzzled look and rattled off more French. Serge asked, "Where is your fiancé?"

"He's in California and is to join me later," I explained. Serge repeated in French my answer to Luke. It took up a lot of time with me just smiling in the direction of whoever was speaking. Serge was struggling with his English. Luke seemed impatient and was anxious to get answers to his questions. We did a lot of smiling back and forth while attempting to understand one another.

I wished I could understand French; that would make it so much easier to correspond with one another. Also, I would have been able to hear and interpret what everyone passing by was saying.

Time passed quickly and Serge said, "How about Luke and I coming later this evening to show you Paree by night?"

Luke leaned closer and said, "*Ce soir, s'il vous plait,*" ("Tonight, please") with a devilish grin on his face. This caught me by surprise.

A thought occurred to me: *How will it be walking around Paris at night with these two men? Serge was a mature gentleman, but Luke was entirely unpredictable.* I glanced over at Serge who was waiting for my answer. I replied, "Sure, that would be great. I really would like to see the city."

Serge added, "We will join you at the hotel at nine o'clock tonight."

Luke followed with a loud, "Oui, oui!"

They escorted me back to my hotel and this time Luke leaned over to kiss me on one cheek then the other. Serge smiled, repeated the same gesture with a kiss on each cheek saying, "Bonsoir."

I entered the hotel lobby and the male desk clerk greeted me with, "Bonjour, mademoiselle!" He came out from behind the desk, walked with me to the elevator, and rolled back the wire door. I stepped in; he smiled and spoke in English, "Did you have a good day?"

"Yes, I did, thanks." I thought to myself, *I really had a good time. It's hard to imagine I'm really in Paris. However, nine o'clock seems late to be sightseeing. But if I'm to see Paree by night, I guess that's when it begins.*

I lay across the bed for over an hour resting. Since the shower was down the hallway, I threw on my three-quarter length pink robe, grabbed a towel, soap, and underwear and headed for the WC. It was an experience pulling a chain above your head to flush the toilet. The toilet paper was like wax paper. It was refreshing to take a shower; I was careful not to get my hair wet. I returned to my room to pick out my outfit for the evening, slightly anxious about not knowing what to expect that night.

I rang for the little elevator a few minutes before nine. I returned the bellman's smile when he said, "Bonsoir, mademoiselle."

Once in the lobby, I seated myself near the front entrance. Luke and Serge were right on time. Serge kissed me on both cheeks. This time Luke took hold of my hand and assisted me from the chair with his devilish smile. He was behaving more gentlemanly this evening. I thought, *American men could certainly learn a lot from such sweet gestures.*

We walked about a block to Serge's gray Peugeot station wagon. Luke walked on my left side and Serge, between me and the curb. Serge opened the front door on the passenger's side; I slid in and Luke climbed into the backseat behind Serge. We drove down the Champs-Elysees. All the cars only had their parking lights on. Serge drove through the Arch of Triumph which was highlighted with bright flood lights. Serge flashed his headlights on and off.

"Why don't the cars have their headlights on?" I inquired.

"In the city limits of Paris only parking lights are permissible. But tonight we can use full headlights if we wish. Usually we only flash our lights on and off when approaching another car or an intersection," Serge replied.

He pointed out the Louvre, the Eiffel Tower, Maxim's, and Notre Dame. Most landmarks looked magical with spotlights illuminating them. People were shouting from cars, standing up in convertibles, bobbing up from sun roofs and horns were blowing from all cars. I wondered what was going on among the French.

"This is the day of The Bastille, like your 4th of July celebration in the U.S. We are permitted to beep our horns and use our headlights tonight," Serge explained. We parked near the Eiffel Tower and walked to the promenade. The air was sticky warm, heavy laden with humidity. It was crowded with people singing, drinking, holding hands and dancing about.

On our way back toward the car, Serge and Luke continued to exchange in French. Serge translated, "Luke wants to take you to the 'La Mer,' the produce district, to a special restaurant." So, off we headed to see how the produce is brought into the city before daybreak. Truckers were wheeling large carts of carrots, green vegetables, and fruit from their trucks. The vendors all along the street were setting up stands getting ready for early shoppers. It reminded me of the movie "Irma la Douce." We had steak, French fries, and wine. The *pommes frites* were the best French fries I believe I'd ever eaten.

I glanced at my watch; it was four o'clock in the morning.

Serge and Luke exchanged more French as we walked to the car. Serge offered, "Luke has to be at work in a few hours, so I'll drop him near his house not far from Notre Dame."

It wasn't a long distance until Serge pulled over to the curb and stopped. Luke said, *"Bonne nuit,"* with his big smile as he opened the back door to exit. I surprised myself with, "Merci, Luke. I can't thank you enough for such a lovely evening." Serge drove around Notre Dame, pulled to a parking space, and parked. He got out and hurried around to open my door. It was beginning to break day.

"Shall we walk a bit?" he asked, holding his arm out for me take hold.

I answered, "Sure! It's lovely."

We walked along the Seine for about an hour. The mist was rising from the river much as it had the morning when I arrived. Communicating was easier with Luke gone. Serge was speaking English quite well.

Serge drove back to in front of the hotel, turned toward me and said, "Luke wants to meet again for an aperitif around six o'clock."

I hesitated before answering, "Yes, I guess. It's all right." At that moment I thought, *I shouldn't be doing this every night. But I'm really seeing Paris. Paco would not approve, regardless of how innocent this was.*

I felt squeamish when Serge rang the bell for the doorman. After all, I had been out all night with two Frenchmen. Serge held the door as he kissed me on both cheeks, "Au revoir, Joan."

I smiled and said, "Goodnight, Serge." Although it should have been a "Bonsoir," it was too late for me to think in French. It was obvious to the bellman I had been out all night too. He looked back at Serge and gave him a big grin. I waited as he picked up my room key from behind the front desk and followed him to the elevator. Stepping in as he held the wire door open, I thought, *I've not had time to collect my thoughts or make plans since I arrived. Each day surpasses the one before.* I changed into my shorty pajamas and dropped into bed. I was awakened by the chambermaid at three that afternoon. I excused her, grabbed my robe, and went to the W.C. to shower. I hurried to dress, rang for the elevator, and dropped off my key. The Frenchman said, "There's a message from Serge requesting you join him at nine o'clock to see the fireworks."

"Thanks! Merci," I said heading to hit the pavement on my own again. With my small map I headed toward the Opera House. It was so exciting sitting outside at the Opera Café having lunch, watching people come and go. My regret, once again, was not being able to understand the spoken language. My table was typically small with barely enough space for my plate and utensils. I was beginning to understand the French currency and could translate a few more French words. Afterwards, I walked up and down narrow streets window shopping, comparing prices in American money. I was so intrigued I lost sight of the time. I glanced at my watch and it was five o'clock. I hurried back to my hotel to change clothes to meet Luke.

Luke was on time and he escorted me to another sidewalk café. It was more difficult without Serge to translate. We sipped our drinks and returned awkward smiles as we tried to understand one another. It was tiresome and frustrating.

When we were about to leave, Serge showed up. I was relieved to see him. He leaned over and kissed me on both cheeks and pulled up a chair. He related that Luke could not join us for fireworks tonight due to another commitment. Serge ordered a martini, and Luke stayed a short while, speaking rapidly in French to Serge. I didn't understand a word of it. With a sad grin Luke stood up, took hold of my hand, and said, "Bonsoir."

I started to get up, but he motioned for me to stay seated. He looked sad, turned, and walked away. Serge explained, "Luke felt left out since the two of us were able to communicate in English and he couldn't."

"I'm so sorry, Serge. However, I knew how hard it was last evening with Luke sitting in the back seat and you trying to translate back and forth between us."

"It's all right, Joan," Serge replied. "He wishes you the best during your visit." Serge paid the check and helped me up from my chair. Realizing I had seen Luke for the last time, I was relieved somewhat. But I had appreciated his help. I didn't want to tell Serge about his flirtations. It was rather sad knowing Luke's "Bonsoir" meant a final goodbye as well.

"Serge," I said after some thought, "when you see him, please thank him once again for helping me find a hotel."

Serge and I walked a short distance to where his car was parked. He drove around the Arch of Triumph and headed for the Concorde above the city. It was hot and humid, much like a typical Fourth of July in Pennsylvania. We joined a huge crowd of people gathered on the steps leading up to the Concorde. Everyone was celebrating, singing together with drinks in hand and dancing about. Fireworks began shooting over the city. It was brilliant to watch. I could feel the perspiration running down my spine and my underarms were soaked. I dabbed my forehead repeatedly with my handkerchief. The humidity was horrific!

It was early morning when we got back to my hotel. Serge turned toward me and asked, "Shall we plan on an aperitif around five o'clock tonight?"

I paused for a moment, "Well, yes, I guess so." Serge was such a nice man and seemed determined to show me his city. What harm could come of it? I'd been straightforward about Paco. There had been no signs of him trying to make advances toward me as his friend Luke had. Serge had told me of his divorce; other than that, I knew very little about him.

These past few days had been all about Luke and the two of them showing me Paris. Serge opened the car door for me and ran ahead to ring the outside bell of the hotel. He kissed me on both cheeks saying, "*Bonne nuit,* Joan."

I replied with, "Thanks for a lovely evening." I was too tired to think of any French such as *bonsoir*, meaning a "good evening." The bellman escorted me via elevator back to my room. I glanced in the dresser mirror as I entered. There was a wet spot down the back-seam of my beige skirt and the waistband was also soaked from perspiration. Luckily it had been dark at the

Concorde, but I wondered if my wet skirt had been noticeable. It was uncomfortably hot, and I had perspired through my half-slip and silk-lined skirt. I hung my skirt and slip on a hanger to dry. I would have to take my silk-lined skirt to the cleaners.

I slipped into my pajamas and looked out through the open corner windows at the intersection below. An attractive French woman with a short tight skirt and high heels was leaning against a bright red convertible with the top down. It appeared she was a high-class streetwalker making a deal with whomever. She didn't get in the car but walked farther down the narrow street. My windows were both open when I returned. My guess was the maid thought it would be cooler; it wasn't. There was no air conditioning or fan in my room. Another well-dressed woman came into view. It was interesting to watch the activity on the street below, but I couldn't fight sleep any longer and went to bed.

The sun coming in my window awakened me. It was eight o'clock by my travel alarm clock. I was looking forward to another day to explore Paris. Excited I rushed to leave the hotel and find a café for breakfast. I followed the map the front desk clerk gave me to reach the American Embassy. I glanced at the jobs available for 500 Francs which would be about $125.00 in American money. The thought of living and working in Paris was intriguing. It would be better than returning to selling telephones in Hollywood. But what about Paco? Am I so excited with Paris I've forgotten why I'm here? He would not be pleased with my association with Serge or my running around Paris alone, even though Serge had been so kind and such a gentleman. There was no way I could have seen Paris to this extent without Serge and Luke escorting me. Regardless, if Paco knew about Serge and Luke accompanying me around, he would find it unacceptable. He would not take it lightly.

I found the Galleries Lafayette I'd heard so much about in the states. Everything was expensive. A small jar of Pond's cold cream was six francs (equivalent to about $1.30) in Paris. I could probably get the same jar for fifty cents at home. The store was bright and beautiful. I got lost roaming around the floors. Clothes were more expensive than in California and I was on a budget.

I walked to the West Bank. The artists were friendly with a "Bonjour, mademoiselle!" and numerous pleasant nods from those not glued to their canvas. I pondered over buying an oil of a Paris street scene which was well done. Realizing there was no way I could carry it around with me. I declined to buy it. I walked past Maxim's and stopped for a picture, realizing how famous it was. When I got back to my hotel I had just enough time to freshen up to meet Serge.

Serge was prompt and wearing a gray business suit, white shirt, gray tie, and black, narrow-toed shoes needing some polish. I asked, "Is there a place nearby where I can price a car? It would be great to find transportation to drive down to Germany to visit my friend, Jan." He led me to where his car was parked and drove me to the Citroen dealer. Even the weird-looking small car in the showroom with only four cylinders was over seventeen hundred American dollars.

"If I buy a car this expensive, it will take away from the money I have to travel. Serge, I've come this far and want to see as much of Europe as possible en route to my final destination, Barcelona."

Serge smiled, "I understand. What about that?" He pointed to a new Vespa jokingly in the show room window near where we parked. I laughed, "I wouldn't get very far, since I've never driven one." We stopped at another café for a martini. I really was becoming fond of these sidewalk cafés.

As we entered my hotel lobby, I noticed a look of approval from the desk clerk to Serge.

"Bonsoir," he said, kissing me again on both cheeks. I was beginning to like the way the Frenchman addressed women. And now I was no exception.

It was the next morning when I dropped my room key off at the front desk. The clerk said in English, "These two Frenchmen are asking if they could show you 'Paree by Night.'" I looked up with a half-smile at the two men standing with wide grins from ear to ear by the front desk.

"Tell them thanks, but I've seen it!" I thought, *If the looks on their faces are an indication of their intent, I imagine they want to show me more than just "Paree."* I turned and headed for the door to start another day of adventure.

After breakfast I headed to the metro to find the right subway to the Eiffel Tower. My plan was to ride to the top. The large map by the ticket booth showed the metro lines in different colors. It was easy to plan where to get on, off, or to transfer. The subway cars had huge rubber wheels, different from those in New York. I made it to Trocadero station and had a small walk to the tower. I bought a ticket to the top. It was a warm and cloudy day. The visibility of the city wasn't perfect. I accidentally broke a fingernail positioning my camera for pictures. The nail fell over the railing. I looked down remembering tales of things falling from the top of tall buildings hurting someone way below. I chuckled to myself—hoping it didn't hit anyone down there. I hated losing my index fingernail.

Using the metro again, I rode to the nearby museum at the Petit Palais and spent a couple of hours viewing paintings by artists like Renoir with whom I was familiar. There were mosaics on display from the second century.

My last stop was the Bastille. The blister that had formed on my big toe was beginning to be bothersome. I checked the soles of my shoes and the leather was worn through. It was no wonder; I'd been hitting the pavement and exploring the streets of Paris for almost two weeks.

Back in my room, I heard an unexpected rap on the door. The bellman said, "A gentlemen is asking for you in the lobby." I followed him to the elevator and down to the lobby. Serge stepped forward to kiss me on both cheeks saying, "Bonjour." I was surprised; I smiled and glanced up at the clock behind the front desk. I had lost sight of how late it was.

"I'm really tired this evening do you mind if I skip tonight?" I asked meekly. "My hair needs washing and I've walked all over Paris today. My feet are killing me."

Serge accepted my apology with, "It's fine. I'm off tomorrow. How about meeting for breakfast and I'll take you anywhere you wish?"

"Thanks, Serge," I said with relief. "Let's not make it too early. How about after 8:30?" He nodded in agreement. Walking to the elevator, I thought, *He's such a sincere and polite French gentleman.*

The following morning I was a few minutes late. Serge was waiting in the lobby and greeted me with his usual kisses. I thought, *I'm going to really miss all this attention back in America.*

"Is there a post office nearby to send some post cards to the U.S.?" I asked.

"Of course, Joan. I'll take you there," he responded.

What an experience standing in line trying to mail a few postcards. The postal workers weigh and measure each card. The cost was equal to an American dollar or more for each one. After this time-consuming and expensive experience, I knew I wouldn't be sending cards as often as I originally thought.

Serge assisted me in calling the train station about their schedule to Wiesbaden, Germany, this coming Sunday. I purchased a first-class ticket at the American Express window.

Serge asked, "Why don't you spend your last weekend at our family cottage in the French countryside. It will give you a chance to see more of France away from the city."

I had just spent almost two weeks with Serge. He showed me more of Paris than I could ever have managed on my own. I didn't hesitate to reply, "I would like to see the countryside. Thanks, that'll be great."

"I'll pick you up at your hotel at noon on Saturday then," he said.

He drove me back to my hotel and there was time left for more sightseeing on my own. I walked to Notre-Dame to see the amazing architecture, including the magnificent rose windows. Waiting in line for a ticket, a young man started talking to me in English. He was from Madrid. I bragged to him, "My boyfriend is from Barcelona and was a professional soccer player."

"What's his name," he inquired.

When I answered, "Paco Hidalgo," he seemed excited.

"I know of him; he was quite an athlete," he offered. With that he grabbed hold of my hand and helped me make my way through the crowd. He started naming the different statues and explaining the displays behind glass. It was dark and damp inside the Chapel. He was knowledgeable and his mannerisms were much like Paco's. I wondered, did he really know of Paco or was this a come-on?

"When in Spain you must visit Madrid. It's a fascinating city," he advised.

"I hope to. My brother was stationed there with the U. S. Air Force. He loved it and sent me pictures and letters from there." I don't know how I happened to run into this man, but he made my trip to Notre-Dame a learning experience and an interesting afternoon. At the end of the tour we departed.

That evening I developed a sore throat and had difficulty sleeping. The next morning my sore throat was worse, and I tried to express my thanks to the chambermaid and could barely talk. It was sad leaving, but I bid my "*Au revoir*" to everyone. The bellman helped me with my bags onto the elevator and to the lobby. I was paying my bill when Serge arrived. The bellman carried my two bags to Serge's car. I handed him a couple of francs and placed my cosmetic bag on the back seat.

It was a nice drive out into the countryside. I responded in a hoarse voice in response to Serge's questions. The cottage was quaint with four small rooms furnished with old-fashioned furniture. I expected to meet members of his family there. The cottage was empty. There was a small metal tank above the kitchen sink. Serge lighted the tank and explained it delivered the hot water. Serge carried my bags to a bedroom.

After settling in, Serge said, "We need to go to the market to purchase food for dinner, Joan." We walked a short distance to a small neighborhood grocer. Serge said, "Pick out some tomatoes for a salad." I began sorting the firmer ones when Serge interrupted me.

"Joan, you need to take some poor ones along with the fresh ones. This helps the owner to be able to stay in business." I complied, but it's not what I would have done in California. Serge chose a long, unwrapped loaf of French bread. While walking the Paris side streets I saw people picking up loaves of unwrapped bread, placing it in their shopping bags or securing it to the back of their bicycles. I thought it was unsanitary, but no one seemed to object to unwrapped bread in France. Serge picked out a beef steak, a chunk of cheese, spinach leaves, some milk and other foods.

Back at the cabin, I helped prepare the salad and set the table. He made homemade mayonnaise dressing as an added touch. The meal was delicious.

After dinner, Serge looked at me intently and said, "Joan, I don't think you really know what you want. Why don't you stay in Paris? Are you really promised to this man, Paco?"

I thought, *What am I in for?* I had not given this visit to the countryside enough prior thought.

"Well, am I promised to Paco? The answer is yes." I continued to explain: "Our agreement was for me to go directly to Barcelona and stay with his mother until Paco arrived. However, I saw this as an opportunity to visit my friend in Germany and see some of Europe at the same time."

"It sounds to me like you are unsure about this man you are in love with." I wanted to tell Serge he was correct and that was why I was making the trip to begin with. To avoid further discussion I began clearing the table, walked to the small sink, and began rinsing the dishes.

"Leave it, Joan," Serge said as he stood. "It's a nice evening for a walk down by the river." He took my arm and led me to the door. Serge was right. The sky was clear. One could make out the constellations. It was cooler than in Paris. The cobble stones were uneven, and I held onto his arm for balance.

As we walked, I said, "Serge, I'm glad you invited me to see the French countryside. It's so relaxing and peaceful here."

After returning to the cottage, we finished the dishes and I said, "If you don't mind, I will turn in for the night. It will be a long day tomorrow to reach Germany."

"No, I don't mind, Joan. Go ahead make yourself comfortable. If you need anything I'll be in the next room."

"*Tres bien, merci,* Serge." I smiled proudly at learning a few words.

He laughed, "If you stayed longer you, would be speaking French for sure."

It was difficult falling asleep that night. Two weeks in Paris were like a whirlwind of images that I couldn't let go of. I drifted off to sleep and suddenly was awakened by a warm body next to mine. I jumped out of the bed. "Serge," I yelled, "what are you doing?"

"I was lonely and wanted to be close."

As I caught my breath, I protested, "This isn't good! I like you very much, but this will not work. I've promised myself to another man and you know that! Now, *please* go back to your room and get some sleep." He slowly crawled out from under the sheet and, without a word, left the room.

In the morning I awoke to the sound of a rooster crowing outside. I freshened up, changed clothes, and greeted Serge in the kitchen. He was preparing breakfast and asked, "How about tea?" I accepted a cup, and he smiled. Not a word was mentioned about what had happened in the middle of the night by either one of us. We had a nice breakfast on a small table outside in his yard. It was a pleasant Sunday morning.

Serge drove me to the Gare du Nord train station. It was busy with people rushing in all directions. Serge carried the two large bags and I had the cosmetic case as we pushed our way through crowds trying to find the right train to Wiesbaden. Serge spoke French to a gentleman who steered us to the correct platform.

Serge stepped onto the train and I followed. He placed my bags in the first compartment on the left. To our surprise, there sat the man from whom Serge got directions earlier. He stood up and shook Serge's hand. "Dr. Ari," he stated by way of introduction.

"I guess we're in the right place to get to Wiesbaden, correct?" I asked with a raspy throat.

"Yes, you made it. We will arrive in the early morning. Please, have a seat," he said with a welcoming wave of his hand.

Before sitting down, I placed my cosmetic case and purse facing the gentleman. I turned to Serge. He was glassy-eyed and, for the first time, gently kissed me on the lips. "Au revoir, Joan," he said gently. "Have a safe journey. It's been fun."

My eyes were tearing also, and I said, "Thanks for everything, my friend. I'll be in touch."

He turned and walked away. I watched out the window as he passed and waved as the train pulled away, picking up speed.

I remained silent, gazing out the window and thinking about all I had seen and done in Paris.

Dr. Ari looked up from his book and said, "You have a bad throat. May I offer you some cognac? It may help soothe it."

He passed a small flask and I took a gulp. "Thanks so much. Are you from Germany?" I inquired.

"No, I'm from the Czech Republic. But I've been living in San Francisco for the past two years," he remarked.

"That's interesting. I've been living near Los Angeles for the past three years, but I was raised in Pennsylvania."

"What brings you so far away? And now onto Germany?" Dr. Ari asked.

I explained my needed vacation, my desire to see Paris, and wanting to visit my good friend living in Wiesbaden. That began a night full of conversation. Dr. Ari explained that he had escaped from Czechoslovakia when the Russians entered at the end of World War II. He had led an interesting life and was on his way to a medical conference. It was a long night made shorter by sharing our life experiences. The train was very comfortable, and I liked the individual compartment. It was more private than the American trains. We arrived at half past seven and Dr. Ari helped me get my bags from the *Bahnhof* (train station) to Bahnhofstrasse where I could store my bags.

"Thanks for helping me with my luggage and enlightening our trip," I said. "Our time together was enjoyable. Have a safe journey, Dr. Ari." We bid our goodbyes.

S.A. AU CAPITAL DE 400.000 F

GARE DE L'EST

72, BOULEVARD DE STRASBOURG
75010 PARIS

TÉL. : 208.40.56

LE NATIONAL
RESTAURANT

3, Place de la Bastille - PARIS (IVe) - Tél. : 272-03-73

No 20.

1 Champignon	450
1 Bordelaise	1100
1 Sorbet	450
1/2 St Loup	500
	2500
	% 380
	2880
1 Menu	1850
TOTAL.....	4730

La direction de l'hôtel
vous souhaite
une bonne nuit

LE FOYER MODERNE : 45, Av. du Gén.-Michel-Bizot, PARIS-XII
Tél. : 307-90-60

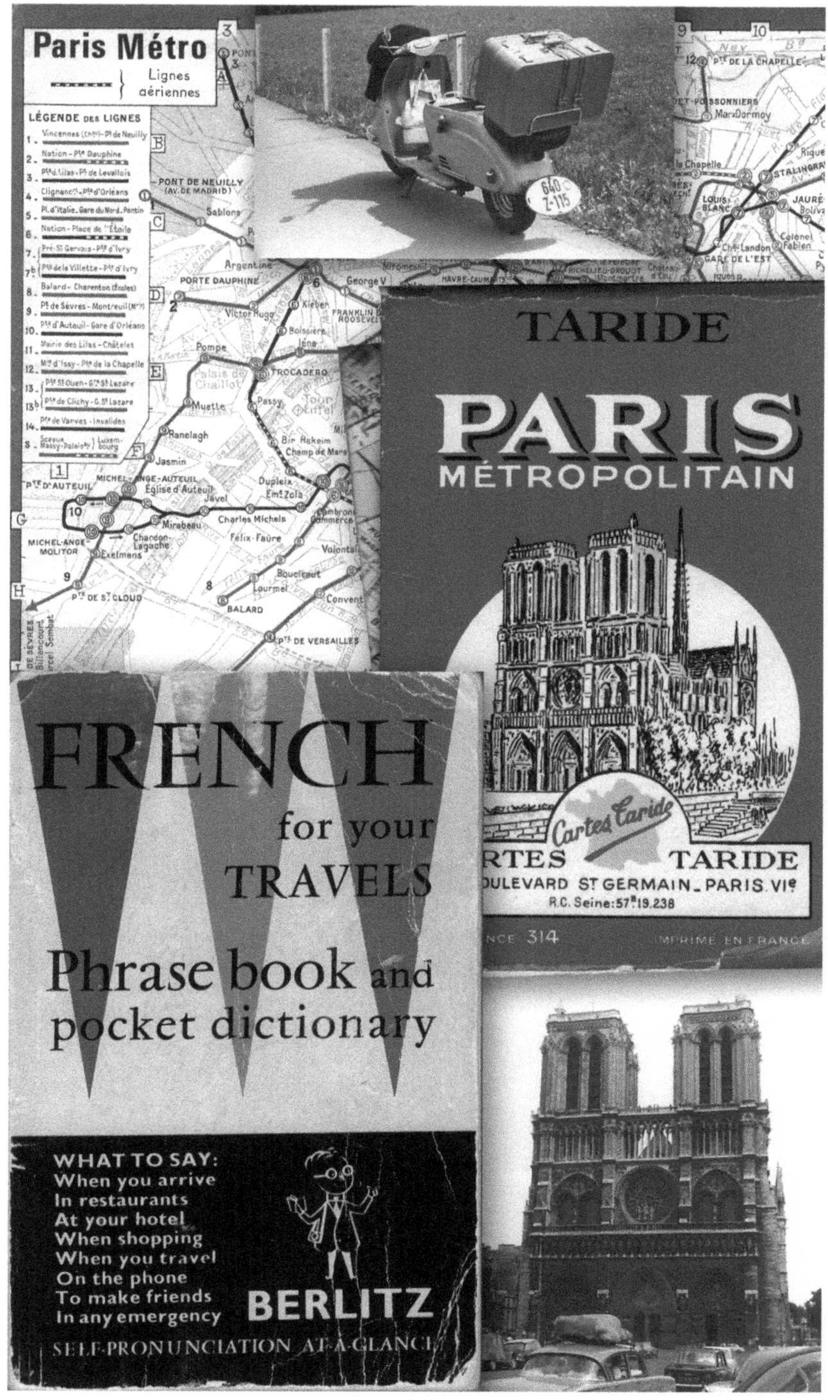
Paris Métro
Lignes aériennes
LÉGENDE DES LIGNES
PONT DE NEUILLY (AV. DE MADRID)
Sablons
Argentine
PORTE DAUPHINE
Victor Hugo
Kléber
Boissière
Iéna
Pompe
TROCADERO
Passy
Muette
Ranelagh
Bir Hakeim
Jasmin
Dupleix
Église d'Auteuil
Javel
Charles Michels
Mirabeau
Félix Faure
Exelmans
MICHEL-ANGE MOLITOR
Boucicaut
Lourmel
BALARD
Convent
Pte DE VERSAILLES
Pte DE St CLOUD
Pte D'AUTEUIL
George V
Pte DE LA CHAPELLE
Marx Dormoy
La Chapelle
LOUIS BLANC
STALINGRAD
Colonel Fabien
GARE DE L'EST
640 Z 115
TARIDE
PARIS
MÉTROPOLITAIN
Cartes Taride
RTES TARIDE
ULEVARD St GERMAIN_PARIS VIe
R.C. Seine:57B19.238
314
IMPRIMÉ EN FRANCE
FRENCH
for your
TRAVELS
Phrase book and
pocket dictionary
WHAT TO SAY:
When you arrive
In restaurants
At your hotel
When shopping
When you travel
On the phone
To make friends
In any emergency
BERLITZ
SELF-PRONUNCIATION AT-A-GLANCE

HOTEL DES CAPUCINES
ANGLE RUE DE SÈZE
6, Rue Godot-de-Mauroy - PARIS (9e)
ADR. TÉLÉGR. CAPUCINOTEL OPÉRA 06-37-06-38

Dear [illegible], JE SUIS TRÈS BIEN
252 PARIS — La Tour Eiffel.
PAREE EST AMUSANT. THE NIGHT
LIFE IS TERRIFIC. EVERYONE IS FULL
OF FUN. I WAS ONLY HERE 10 MINS
TILL I MET A FRENCHMAN WHO HELPED
ME FIND A HOTEL. FIRST HE TOOK ME
TO COOKS TRAVEL AGENCY. HE COULDNT SPEAK
A WORD OF ENGLISH. I HAD LEFT MY
BOOK ON THE PLANE. WHAT AN EXPERIENCE
THINKING OF ONLY A FEW WORDS I
KNEW. YESTERDAY SEEMED LIKE
A MONTH SINCE I WAS TAKEN A
TOUR BY HIS CAR TO NOTRE DAME
EIFFEL TOWER. I STOOD UNDER-NEATH
IT. ATE + DRANK IN CAFÉS. WENT
TO BED AT 5 AM this morning. THEY
HAVE A NATIONAL HOLIDAY TODAY. I'm
going to see the fireworks tonite.
with my two FRENCHMEN. ONE SPEAKS
SOME ENGLISH SO HE INTERPRETS FOR ME.
ADDRESS) HOTEL DES CAPUCINES
6 RUE GODOT-de-MAUROY
PARIS (9e) FRANCE
I'LL WRITE LATER Joan

Éditions GREFF 18 X 20, Faubourg du Temple - Fabrication Française - Reproduction

POSTES VITTEL 0,85 RÉPUBLIQUE FRANÇAISE
PAR AVION

LESS R. FOOR
2654 NEWELL STREET
LOS ANGELES 39, CALIF
U.S.A.

Chapter Three: Wiesbaden, Germany

I left the train station area headed on a journey to find my friend, Jan, in the heart of Wiesbaden, Germany. I questioned several people showing them my map. Lucky for me several Germans spoke English and steered me to the right building. I walked upstairs to the second floor and asked for Jan. The front desk receptionist said, "Janis will be right with you."

"Joan, you're here! I can't believe you did it! How was Paris?" Jan greeted me with a big bear hug.

"It was fantastic! You look great, Jan." Her hair was highlighted blonde—the same as in California. She was fair skinned, about five feet, six inches tall, of average weight, and quite attractive.

"I'll take an early break for lunch and get you settled in," she announced.

It was convenient that my bags were not that far away from her office. We walked over to the baggage claim. After retrieving my bags, Jan carried my large bag and I managed with the other two. It was several blocks to her apartment building.

I noticed sheets and bedding hanging from window sills along the street. Jan remarked, "The frau's air out their linens every day." We stopped to rest a few times on our way. The worst part was lugging the suitcases up five flights of stairs to her flat. She showed me where to put my bags, saying, "Make yourself at home. The couch makes into a bed. I'll be back after five. Help yourself to snacks, anything you can find. The toilet and shower are down the hall, one floor lower. Stay out of the way of

Frau Goring, the owner on the third floor. She complains when we have guests. She even yells out loud in front of everyone, 'I rented to two people only.'"

That evening Jan introduced me to her roommate, Fran, from Brooklyn. Fran was tall, thin, with a full head of black hair teased about her face. Her heavy black eyebrows and complexion looked Hawaiian or Puerto Rican, and she was soft spoken. Several guys arrived from the U.S Air Force Base. We went out for pizza and prosted several beers.

Sure enough, Frau Goring yelled at us when we returned. "You are making too much noise." We were trying to sneak up the stairs holding our hands over our mouths but laughing even more.

Later, Fran and Jan took me to a German Gasthaus. Jan said, "In Germany, you have to drink a Schnapps before each beer. That's the custom." I thought it strange but followed their instructions. I didn't like the taste of Schnapps, but I downed a shot before enjoying several beers. Before long, I was singing and dancing happily. It was a blast! When we returned to Jan's apartment building, she put her finger up to her lips indicating that we were to be quiet going up the stairs past Frau Goring's flat. It was four o'clock in the morning, and we giggled quietly to the fifth floor.

I awoke later that morning with a terrible hangover. Fran started laughing as she got a couple of aspirins for me. That's when she explained, "They were kidding about having to drink a Schnapps before your beer."

"What?" I exclaimed. "You mean to tell me it was a joke? How can anyone like that stuff? No wonder I have a headache!"

"Yes, it was so funny. We had a hard time keeping a straight face. When we turned away Jan and I were cracking up. You took it so seriously."

"I'm glad you all had a fun time watching me. It's an experience I won't forget," I added. Each drink I was served the bar tender placed a pencil stroke onto the coaster under my glass. When I asked for my bill, I paid in German marks according to the number of strokes that appeared on my coaster. It was an honor system, and I guess it works. It was fun singing "Oom-pa-pa with the guy in lederhosen playing an accordion.

The next morning Jan and Fran went off to work. I took my time with going downstairs to the shower and toilet. I noticed the kitchen sink was used to put on makeup, fix one's hair, and for doing dishes. Not having a bathroom or toilet in your apartment would take some getting accustomed to. I ventured out to the Poste. The cost to send a telegram was 32 marks, about eight American dollars. I decided to send cards to notify Paco and Aunt Anna of my address: Joan Foor, c/o Janis Hunt, Hauptpostlagernd, Wiesbaden, Germany. Jan said it was okay to use her address to get mail while I was traveling.

That evening Fran introduced me to her boyfriend, Jerry. We had drinks and snacks before taking a ride in Jan's 1951 Mercedes with no side windows. It was fun riding in the old car—not that it helped my cold much. We visited until early the next morning. I don't know how the girls keep up without getting much sleep. I was glad I could sleep in, because my cough was getting worse.

Jan said, "Try to keep out of Frau Goring's way. If she asks if you are staying here, tell her just a few days. She will complain that the flat is only for two people and we aren't paying rent for more than that. We try to stay out of her way. She doesn't like us bringing our friends in, and you heard how she yells at us when we're having a good time."

I walked gingerly down the stairs past Frau's flat. I walked to the Bahnhof and took a train to Frankfurt. Compared to Wiesbaden, Frankfurt was a large bustling city with people, cars, motorcycles, and trolleys going every direction. After experiencing so many people riding motor scooters in the city I got an idea that perhaps that was a way I could travel. I read the signs which didn't mean much, but I followed my map to Kleyerstrasse. I found the motor scooter dealer, Ernst Heinkel Kundendienst. I looked at new scooters in the showroom. They were too expensive, but I found them interesting.

He had a used, large, metallic-blue Heinkel scooter with a luggage rack over the spare tire. It had a place for a purse to hang in front of the seat and a rack big enough for my cosmetic case over the front headlight. The double seat was on hinges, and underneath was a deep storage space to be used for whatever. I was excited thinking this could serve my purpose. The price was nine hundred marks (less than three hundred U.S. dollars), which I could afford. The thought of driving it didn't occur to me. Apparently, the dealer was selling it on behalf of a private party. He spoke broken English. I wrote a note in English offering 800 marks and mentioned I would return the next day to see if there was an agreement on price.

I walked back toward the train station and passed a *coiffeur*, a beauty parlor. I requested a shampoo and set. The staff spoke no English but understood enough that I received a wash and set for seven marks. They continued conversations in German among each other, and I smiled but understood none of it. The result was good.

I boarded a bus back to Wiesbaden with the great news. I now knew exactly how I would get around Europe reasonably.

That evening, the moment Jan came in the door, I said, "Guess what happened? I made an offer on a Heinkel motor scooter in Frankfurt."

"You did what? Do you know how to drive one?" Jan asked.

"No. But I don't believe it would be difficult. Besides, it will hold my suitcases and I can afford it at eight hundred marks."

Jan looked worried and replied, "I'm concerned about your traveling around Europe on one of those alone."

"I'm sure it'll be fine, and I'm looking forward to being out in the open air."

"Well, it will be interesting, to say the least, to see you on a scooter," Jan remarked.

That evening I met Fred, a friend of Fran's. We walked to another apartment building to meet Edith who worked at the U.S. Air Force library. They called her "Grandma." We had cognac in coffee and another fun evening until early morning.

We tried to walk quietly up the stairs passed Frau Goring's but were giggling too loud and one of the steps creaked. Frau

Goring opened her door in her night gown and demanded, "Who's going there? How many times have I told you no visitors this time of night?"

We hurried to Jan's flat and closed the door laughing. Our sides were hurting from holding back our laughter while climbing the stairs. It continues to amaze me how everyone made it off to work in the morning when they get so little sleep.

Morning came a bit quickly for everyone. I hurried back to the train and over to Frankfurt to see if my offer was accepted. I arrived at 8:45 a.m. and could tell by their expression it was a deal. I paid the eight hundred marks and purchased international insurance. I was excited to realize I now had a way to get around Europe. It was explained that I could drive with temporary papers until I purchased "Sol" plates which were round license plates for Americans. I crawled onto the seat of my scooter. My skirt was too tight! There was no way to reach the brake without pulling my skirt up to my hips. I was disappointed I was unable to drive my new toy to Jan's. I didn't realize how heavy the scooter was until I straddled it. Both of my feet had to be securely on the ground to keep it upright. The dealer was understanding and agreed to keep it until I returned in slacks.

The next morning I was ready to try her out in slacks. I listened to brief instructions about the clutch to switch gears and the accelerator on the handlebars. She had more power than I realized. I engaged the clutch and gave it gas, and it took off. What a thrill heading up the street! By mistake I drove through a trolley stop. People were shouting "*Verboten!*" and waving their arms but I was already in the middle of the trolley tracks and had to keep on going. Luckily for me, no trolleys were coming toward me to pick up passengers on the media strip. I was overly excited from everyone screaming and my trying to engage the clutch that I stalled out after exiting the trolley tracks. I stood there balancing it with both feet on the ground. A young man came over speaking German and pushed me from behind. It started quickly, and I headed for the autobahn.

Once on the highway I clashed the gears several times but

did get up to a speed of eighty kilometers per hour (km/h). A truck of U.S. Army soldiers on my left were waving at me. One of them yelled, "Way to go, girl." I took a glance in their direction but was fighting the wind and trying to keep in my lane. I did chuckle to myself, because this was a first. Here I was driving a two-wheeled vehicle in Germany, and I had never driven one before. My new toy got me to Wiesbaden. I found the place that issued license plates, purchased my "Sol" plate, and used my nail file to secure the plate to the rear fender under the luggage rack.

I parked my scooter on the dirt strip along the street in front of Jan's apartment. When Jan came home, I grabbed her arm, "C'mon, I want you to see my new mode of transportation."

"Take me for a ride," she said.

I quickly responded, "No, I don't feel that comfortable yet."

Jerry, her friend, came by. Without hesitation he jumped onto the seat and, with both feet on the ground, pulled it back from its stand. He said, "Give me the key, Joan. Jan, hop on and let's take it for a spin." Pushing with his feet he guided it down from the curb and Jan climbed behind him placing her arms around his waist. He took off fast. When they were out of sight, I worried about something happening to my new means of transportation. I was relieved when they brought it back intact. They were laughing and apparently got a kick out of it. They made no mention about doubts of my being able to travel via my scooter.

That evening Jan, Fran, Edith (Grandma) and I went to Obermeyers to prost beers. A young German called me "Miss America"—that is, after he had had several beers. We sang along with the accordion and didn't leave until closing. I hit the bed after four o'clock in the morning again. My sore throat was improving probably due to numbing it with beer and wine.

I awoke with another hangover. Fred, Fran's friend, arrived to take us to the U.S. Air Force Base Exchange. Fran and Jan rode with Fred. I followed on my scooter to get more accustomed to its handling. We went to the grill for lunch. I was hungry for an American-style hamburger. I bought a pair of black leather gloves to help avoid more blisters from engaging the clutch on the handlebar. It had been weeks since I had American food. When we got back to the parking lot, Fred's car had been broken into.

"My purse is gone!" Jan yelled back over her shoulder while searching frantically in the back seat. She had received her paycheck of over two hundred dollars. Her purse with passport, keys, and money were gone. For two hours we hunted around the bushes, cars, and trashcans. Our hope was that the thief would take the cash and throw her purse in the trash or bushes. Fred and Jan went to the Air Force police to report the theft. Fran and I continued to search around the parking lot. We all went back to Jan's flat disappointed.

Fred returned at ten o'clock that evening, and drove us to Rudesheim, a small town along the Rhine River. He wanted to cheer us up, especially Jan. We visited the quaint wine cellars, danced, and drank the night away. I was given a small green lantern with a dry cell battery to wear. I tucked the battery in my bra with the little green lantern lit up at my V-neckline. When you wore a green lantern, it meant you were open to accepting an offer for a dance. We left at four o'clock in the morning and arrived back at the flat at five. Chet, a friend of Fran's, was waiting at the flat and took us out for coffee. It was quite a night—I got to bed at six thirty, around the break of day.

Jan awakened me at one o'clock that afternoon wanting another ride on my scooter. She sat on the seat behind me and I drove around a few blocks. I was beginning to feel more secure driving. Jerry her boyfriend and his friend came to hot wire Jan's '51 Mercedes since her keys were stolen. They couldn't get it started. Jerry agreed to take Jan and me to the U.S. Air Force Base to do our laundry. When we returned, I washed out some delicate things and began packing. I loaned Jan some money to carry her over until her next pay day. I felt sad about leaving the next day, but at the same time excited to head for Switzerland. We said our goodbyes before I hit the couch.

Chapter Four: Heidelberg to Switzerland

It was early morning when I drove my scooter into town. I purchased elastic straps to be able to secure my suitcases to the luggage rack. I made a couple of trips to Jan's flat to pick up my luggage. I secured the two larger bags on the rack over the spare tire. My cosmetic case fit perfectly on the small frame over the front fender.

My first stop was Heidelberg. I drove past the castle and found it hard to believe I was there. It looked just like the pictures I had seen on travel brochures. The next stop was Baden Baden, Germany, where I drove into an area of loose gravel and upset my scooter. It was so heavy, I struggled to get it halfway upright. Two men came to help me. Just as they arrived, I managed to get it upright. I thanked them and drove to a Gasthaus, where I checked in for the night. The room was okay, but the shower had a lot to be desired.

I dressed for dinner, got a sandwich, and drank two beers. Feeling a bit tipsy, I walked outside to move my scooter under a carport. It had started to rain. I had traveled only one hundred kilometers that day due to light rain. My hope was to make it to Switzerland the next day.

I loaded my bags early and noticed some oil leaking from my transmission. Dumping it into the shale yesterday must have bent the housing. I drove to a motorcycle garage in Koppenheim, and the men were very kind; it only cost five marks to stop the leak. Riding on toward Switzerland, I ran into heavy winds and rain. I pulled into a barn along the road, filled with hay. Two men on motorbikes came along speaking broken English and led me to another Gasthaus. After checking in, I removed my wet clothes and hung them to dry. I lay down since the wind and rain against my face made me tired. I didn't awaken for fifteen hours; I didn't realize I missed eating dinner.

The next morning I headed out early toward Basel, Switzerland, and continued driving into the city of Zurich which was bustling with traffic. The scenery was greener than Pennsylvania— if that's possible! The mountains were high and the roads dangerously narrow. I didn't have any spills, but it was scary. The Alps were beautiful, but the switchbacks were difficult to steer, going slowly and leaning in around the curves. I stopped at a small hotel along the San Bernadine Pass. Nobody spoke English so I pointed to items on the menu. It was interesting, as the food came up to the dining room via a dumbwaiter. I ordered steak and noodles, salad, coke and ice cream. I expected them to serve Swiss cheese, but it didn't happen. When I turned in for the night, I noticed my face was red from the cold and windburn I'd endured. I realized they had no heat and wore two sweaters to bed.

I was awakened by the sound of a bass-sounding bell. I looked out the window and saw a cow with a large bell around its neck, walking along the hill behind the hotel. Excited for a new adventure I got dressed, ate breakfast, and went outside to check the temperature. Before I left my room, I put on two sweaters to help keep warm. It was a clear, beautiful, crisp morning. I needed more than my leather gloves and scarf around my head. The steep pass kept spiraling upward, one turn after another. Suddenly, I couldn't turn sharp enough around a curve and ran into a wall. I lost control of the scooter and dumped it. Fortunately, I pulled my leg out of the way just in time before it hit the ground. A man following me in a diesel truck came to my aid. He lifted the scooter from the dirt and got it upright.

This was no time to ponder getting back on my scooter. I needed to master it and take better control of the vehicle. I climbed back on the seat and drove until I found a plateau area.

The Alps were snow-covered and presented one of the most beautiful sights I'd ever seen. I found a tree and pulled my scooter back on its stand. I ran along the edge of the road ahead looking down. I snapped some pictures, wishing I had more film. As I looked through the lens, it reminded me of the panoramic opening view of the movie "The Sound of Music." I ran out from the road looking down and started singing, "The hills are alive with the sound of music!" My voice echoed right back. What an experience! I followed with, "Climb every mountain, ford every stream, follow every rainbow till you find your dream." I was singing from my heart. My audience was the Alps with an echo that was incredibly inspirational.

I walked back to my Heinkel and headed happily down the winding road, hoping it would be easier going downhill. It wasn't. The wide turns and tunnels on my way to Italy were just as dangerous. I began to wish with every curve that it would lead to a more level road. I made it to Bellouza, Switzerland, in one piece. Farmers were turning hay along the road. They waved and I waved back. There were small interesting farmhouses and hay barns. I thought, *It would be exciting to stay as a farm hand for the experience.* However, I knew I must keep driving toward Spain.

What a relief to be out of the Alps. I promised myself to never go through the Alps again on a motor scooter!

Chapter 5: Italy

Friday, July 31st, I arrived in Italy. Dinner was not available until late, after nine o'clock in the evening; the wine went straight to my head. I ordered beef with tomatoes, and fruit for dessert. They brought me a bowl of water with the fruit. The custom is that you wash your own fruit at the table—interesting! Driving around these roads I felt more at home because there were lots of motor scooters, especially Vespas, going all directions. The women were sitting behind the driver, seated sideways. Some had a wrap over their legs and others exposed their legs to the side.

After passing Aleona, I realized I was about halfway to Rome. At the gas station along the highway, they wouldn't accept my German marks. I handed over fifty marks. "I'll be back," I said. I got back on my scooter, drove up the road to a restaurant where they exchanged some marks to lire. When I got back to the gas station I demanded, "Give me back my marks and I'll give you lire." They did it and chuckled at my demeaner.

To that point, everyone was very friendly and seemed to be happy. I never saw so many motor bikes, scooters and bicycles going in all directions. I passed a sign that read "Roma." I was somewhere between Forli and Perugia. A young man waved his arms and flagged me down. I pulled over thinking maybe one of my tires were low or my suitcases were shifting from the rack in back. I quickly walked around my scooter and found nothing visibly wrong. His Italian language sounded urgent. I lifted my seat up and pulled out my French Berlitz dictionary. He smiled as I pointed out French words as an attempt to communicate. We stood alongside of the road turning pages in my dictionary. It was funny that there was nothing wrong. He had never seen a Heinkel motor scooter before or a woman driving a scooter on a country road. At least this was my impression as he walked all around the scooter. He introduced himself as "Charles."

I followed along behind his Fiat which made it easier for me. He flagged me down two times along the way, first for ice cream and later to a café where I purchased a coke. He picked up the check, which was great for I wasn't certain yet of the exchange rate from American or German dollars to lire. I had already experienced a lot of big lira bills in exchange for German marks at the gas station. I didn't have time to check my American Express Currency Converter to figure out the exchange rate.

He finally led me to a hotel north of Rome with the sign "La Perla." It was very pleasant and seamed reasonably priced. Charles helped with my luggage through an open security gate leading to an outside stairwell to the second floor. As I opened the door he pointed to his watch. My interpretation was that he would return in about two hours.

Sure enough, a couple of hours later I heard a knock on my door. He led me to where his Fiat was parked. His car was tiny with a soft top rolled back. Charles held the door for me to get in. Here I was, in another situation where I had to decide whether to get in or not. I thought, Why not? *It's broad daylight and he seems like a gentleman.* I got in, and off we went. The breeze felt inviting, and I loved sightseeing and exploring. We didn't share much conversation other than his pointing out landmarks along the way.

Charles drove slowly around a curve. In front of us were a couple of twenty-foot-tall, large wooden doors, now open, leading toward a steep, extremely narrow road to Assisi. These tall, thick doors were used to block the road up the hill to the city in previous times. We walked around the shops and stopped every now and then to look at some words in my French dictionary. Once again, I was at a disadvantage not being able to speak another language. It took a lot of time to translate a word or two at a time. And I found out one lira was worth two cents in American money.

Charles drove me back to the hotel and turned on his Italian charm at the doorway to my room. I smiled and said, "Thank you for a nice day." I quickly shut my door. I cleaned up, changed clothes, and went to the restaurant before going to bed.

An unexpected knock on my hotel door startled me. It had to be about midnight, I cautiously went to the door. "Who is it?" I called out.

"*Sono io,* Charles," was the muffled response.

"No, no, Charles. I'm ready for bed." Whether or not he understood what I was saying was questionable.

He knocked louder and insisted, "Signora Joan, *per favor. Fammi entrare!*"

I walked closer to the door and said, "Charles, go away. I'm ready for bed."

He was beginning to scare me. I had no telephone in my room to call downstairs. I thought, *How did he get up to the second floor and my room this time of night?*

He pounded rapidly with what sounded like his fist. "Charles, let me alone!" I yelled out loud. "Please go away!"

Someone surely would hear me and make him go away. With my ear against the door it sounded like he was going down the steps. It was difficult to get back to sleep wondering what got into him. He was such a gentleman during the day. It was scary. He must have had a few drinks before the pounding began. Someone had to have given him access to that gate leading up the outside stairwell to my room. Lord knows what story he gave the staff to get access. Of course, I realized, this was Italy. I reflected upon my last conversation with Paco, and his pronouncement: "A woman should not be traveling alone in Europe." I would need to be more cautious in the future.

On August 2nd, Sunday, I paid my bill after breakfast, secured my suitcases into place on the scooter, and headed for Rome. Approaching the city, I felt at home with the other scooters, mostly Vespas and Lambrettas, traveling on both sides of me. The swirling traffic circles were the worse. I had to drive around the circle several times to get access to the far-right lane to exit. It was dangerous and made me nervous. I could see the Colosseum and other famous landmarks as I drove frantically round and round, trying to find a place to park. Disappointed, I was forced into continuing along the road leading outside the city. Other riders on scooters waved, shouted out, or stared as I drove past. It was apparent they had not seen a woman alone on a strange-looking scooter with all her possessions aboard.

Ten kilometers later, I found the Grand Hotel in Frascati, which was plush. What a relief to be able to lessen the grip on my handlebars. I unloaded my bags, unpacked, and was delighted to have a full bath and toilet adjoining my room. After a bubble bath and change of clothing—which transformed me—I went to the restaurant. Lasagna, salad, and a beer on the menu required no translation. I followed that with spumoni. I began to think about a sightseeing day tomorrow in Rome on my scooter without baggage.

I discovered there was so much to see, and one day was not enough to encompass the history of Rome. I took pictures as I toured the Colosseum, the largest Roman amphitheater in the world. As I looked down, it was easy to imagine the gory battles between men, animals and carriages. I pictured some of the scenes in my mind from the movie *Ben Hur.* I drove past the Pantheon wanting to stop, but I knew I needed to head for Pisa by two o'clock that afternoon to arrive before dark. I drove back to my hotel and loaded my baggage onto the scooter.

Traveling by scooter had to be during daylight hours, considering I was not familiar with roads and terrain. Each day I wrote down the major cities I would travel through on my way to the destination I chose. This list I secured under the strap holding my cosmetic case in place on the rack over my front fender, under my handlebars. It was easy to see while traveling. On average, I planned a TripTic of 350–450 kilometers.

Not paying attention one day, I sputtered out of gas. Luckily a man helped me push the scooter a block to a gas station. I began searching for a hotel, eventually winding up the hills. I stopped at one hotel; it was full. The air was getting chilly and it was almost dark. I turned around, heading out of the hills. At the bottom I asked a young man crossing the street, "Where is a hotel?" He pointed to a building that didn't look like a hotel. Lucky for me, they rented out rooms. I was relieved, for it was almost pitch-black outside.

When I entered the restaurant that evening, I heard some people speaking English. My ears perked up for I had not heard English for days. A gentleman introduced himself as Renardo from Rome. We talked back and forth between tables. It was fun talking in English during and after dinner. But he reminded me of the "Charles" character I met outside of Rome who pounded on my door after midnight. I was extremely careful not to encourage him.

This small town was like a ghost town. It was cold due to the altitude and located by the Italian coast. When I drove out of the hills, I was shivering from the cold hoping not to get a cold like the one I had in Paris. I went up to my room about eleven o'clock that night.

At about half-past midnight, I heard an argument going on. A few minutes passed and I was startled with a knock on my door. I opened the door part way and there was Renardo standing with a Coca-Cola for me. I thought, *These Italian men sure are persistent. At least this one speaks English.* He grabbed hold of my arm and pulled me out of the doorway. He led me downstairs to the café. I was in my pajamas; thank heavens they were heavy ones. After a second coke, I convinced him I had to get some rest before the long day I planned for tomorrow. He was attractive and I enjoyed being able to speak English for a change. He began to turn on the charm and tried his best to lure me into a romantic encounter, but I was on the alert! It wasn't going to happen.

On Tuesday, August 4th, I took my scooter into a service shop. I saw several Vespas, other motorcycles and scooters in the garage. I wanted to be sure the transmission wasn't leaking, and overall it was running okay. The scooter seemed ready for the trip, so I headed for Pisa, Italy. I drove around the city looking for a high tower. I didn't see anything and headed up a grade and looked down onto the city. Nothing resembled a tower. I got back on board and drove into the center of Pisa. I found the leaning tower with tourists circling around it. It was leaning but much shorter than I expected; no wonder I hadn't found it earlier. I parked my scooter where I could sit down at a café across the street. After a sandwich and an aperitif, I walked around it but didn't take the tour inside.

I left Pisa and drove farther up the coast toward La Spezia; I stopped at Rapallo. I browsed in and out of interesting shops then stopped for ice-cream. The views driving along the rocky coast of Northern Italy were beautiful. It was hard to keep my eyes only on the road. I drove along a two-lane coastal highway. The traffic came to a halt in front of me. Drivers were getting out of their cars and walking around. An English-speaking man walked back my way and told me there was a landslide on the road ahead. He said, "It will be hours until they let us through." Glancing a few cars ahead, I witnessed a whole family walk down from the road to the ocean.

I opened my suitcase and got out a bathing suit. There were some large bushes on the hillside along the road. I walked up and, hiding behind the bushes, changed into my bathing suit. I got my purse out from beneath the seat and climbed down the rocky embankment to the ocean. I sat my purse by a rock and dove in. It was refreshing after sitting on my scooter in the hot sun.

It was only about a half hour when the traffic ahead of me started to move. I grabbed my purse and hurried up to my scooter. I didn't have time to change clothing. I slipped my blouse over my suit and was able to follow the car ahead of me. The traffic was slow-moving along that narrow windy road. I passed the area not long afterwards where they were still clearing up more debris from a rockslide onto the highway.

I continued to drive along the Italian coast until I was getting chilled, even though my bathing suit was now dry. I stopped and slipped on a pair of slacks over my suit. A few miles farther I found a small hotel. I unloaded, cleaned up and changed clothing for dinner.

While dining that evening, I met Lionel from San Francisco who spoke English. We shared the table, lasagna, and wine, which made for several hours of good conversation in my language. It had been a long, interesting day, and I turned in after dinner.

The next morning, my plan was to head toward Monaco. I didn't see Lionel to say goodbye and tell him I enjoyed our visit and conversation. My drive took me onto the Autostrada, Italy's freeway. I held my speed around eighty to eighty-five km/h. I tried to keep out of the way of cars speeding past me.

I arrived at a quaint-looking old harbor that curved around like a horseshoe. Small ships with wooden hauls and square-shaped, canvas sails dotted the bay. The bright afternoon sun reflected a golden glow from the ships' sails against a dark blue sea, making the scene worthy of several camera shots. It reminded me of the old-time movies I had seen of pirate ships. But these were more primitive, ones you would expect to find in a remote area in China.

I pulled away slowly and drove along the curved pavement looking out at the vastness of the Mediterranean Ocean. It inspired a feeling of peacefulness, and it was unique. Small shops facing the bay appeared vacant. When I returned my camera to under my seat, I thought, *I will return here one day.* The town was Genoa, Italy.

My drive along the coast led me to Menton, France, and Hotel Le Vendome. I realized I was now on the southern tip of France and not far from Monaco. I unpacked, showered, and headed for the restaurant, where I ordered French fries. The fries were delicious! The French fries in California could not compete with these. (No wonder we pour ketchup on them.)

A vocalist was singing in French and everyone was joining in. I left for bed at midnight, wondering if I could take a day of rest and spend it on the beach.

I decided to stay a day, and after breakfast I went shopping for a beach towel. The walking shorts for sale were too short for me. I slipped on my bathing suit and walked down the rocky beach to the Mediterranean. The sand was filled with coarse small rocks, so I hurried and dove into the ocean. It was warm, calm, and peaceful. I spent the afternoon sitting on my new beach towel, watching people walk to the ocean and back. Some had little tent-like canopies. These little A-frame-like canvas or cloth canopies shaded most of their bodies from the sun. Some couples were kissing in their little tents.

I suddenly had a flashback of Paco, wished he was beside me. Everything here was more expensive. My dinner last night and this evening was fifteen francs. My hotel and food for two days cost over twenty-five dollars in American currency. It was great to live it up, but I was way over my daily budget. My plan for tomorrow was to head for Monaco, then on to Nice.

On Friday, August 7th, I left Menton at ten o'clock in the morning and arrived at the port of Monaco. The bay was crowded with expensive large and small yachts lined up, side by side. The sun was shining against a clear blue sky with some small white puffy clouds in the distance. It looked just like the picture postcard I bought to send back home. I visited Princess Grace's Castle and pushed my scooter to the front of the castle. It was like another dream I wanted to continue and not wake up from. Here I was, actually standing in front of the castle, and I could look down at the beautiful harbor. I walked alongside my scooter back down to the harbor before I hopped on and headed for Nice, France.

The wind along the coast picked up, and it began to rain. Having no rain gear, I kept driving through the city. The wind and rain were stinging my face and made it difficult to see the road. I had to call it a day at half-past four.

I stopped at a small hotel outside of Aix en Provence. The toilet was interesting, with two steel footprints on the floor, a hole in between, and a tank behind with a chain. When you pulled the chain, the water came from a small tank above your head to flush. This took a balancing act.

The food was deliciously French, but the lights kept flickering on and off in sync with thunder and lightning flashes. Luckily, they had a carport for my Heinkel.

I checked the map and wrote down my destination point as Barcelona, Spain. Approximately one hundred kilometers away, I ran into heavily-flooded roads. The rivers spilled over the highway, making the water level about a foot deep. I watched as cars and trucks drove through the water, making waves which would be higher than my running board. Wanting to push onward, I decided to pick out a large truck and follow close as the water was disbursed by the truck's large wheels. It was a risky maneuver, and I drove close and slow, praying the water would not flow over my feet. It was cold, scary, dangerous, and tense—but it worked! I stopped at seven that evening at a place resembling a motel in the states.

That night I met two girls from Florida who were traveling by car. Once again, it was great to speak English. We talked and laughed at a table for two hours. The customers in the restaurant kept staring at us; I guess we were having too much fun. Dinner cost me four dollars, and at this rate my money would not take me as far as I wanted to go. I knew I must conserve. C'est la Vie!

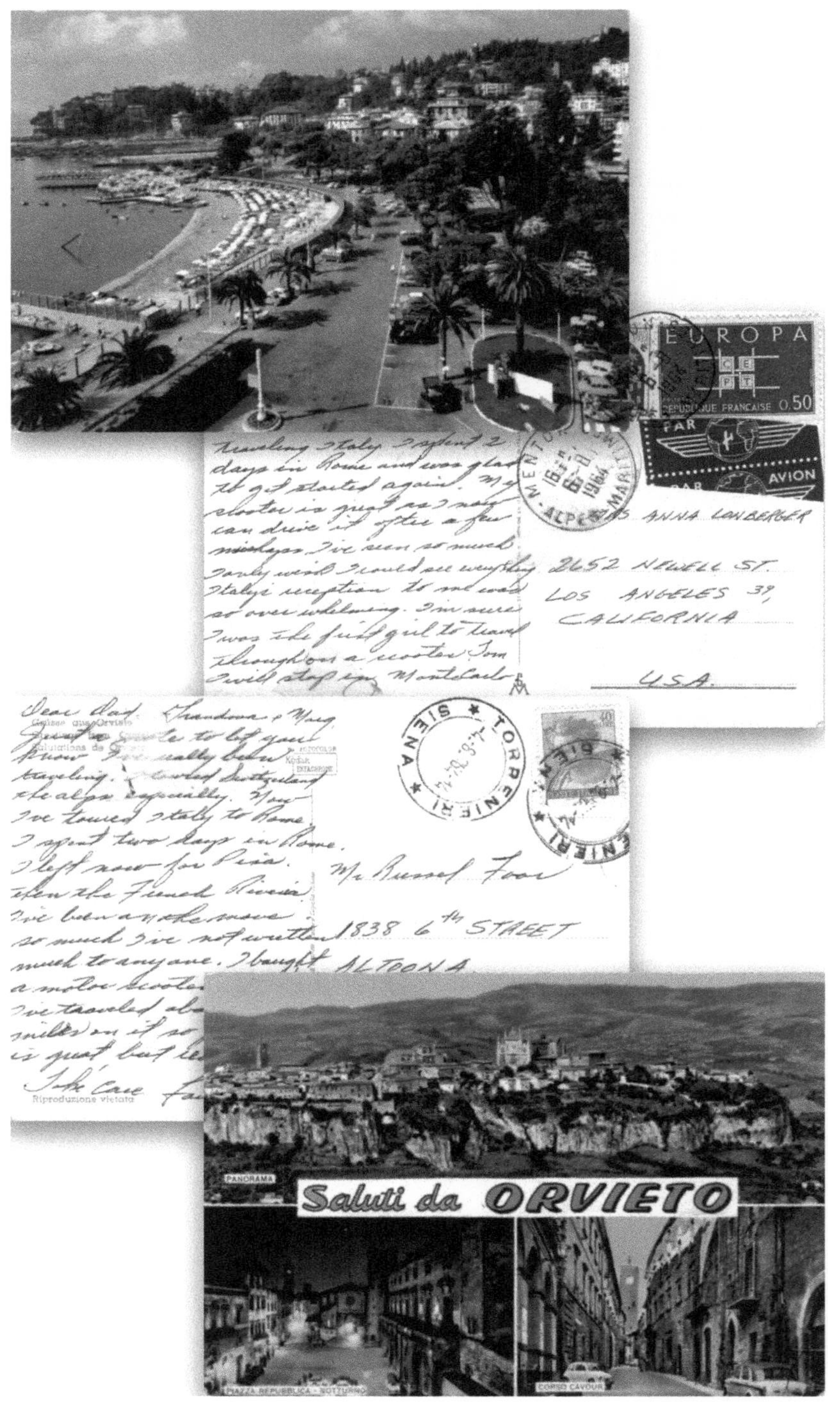
traveling Italy. I spent 2 days in Rome and was glad to get started again. My scooter is great as I now can drive it after a few mishaps. I've seen so much I only wish I could see everything. Italy's reception to me was so overwhelming. I'm sure I was the first girl to travel through on a scooter. Tom I will stop in Montecarlo

MRS ANNA LANBERGER
2652 NEWELL ST.
LOS ANGELES 39,
CALIFORNIA
U.S.A.

Dear Dad, Thanksgiving & May
Just a line to let you know I've really been traveling. I toured Switzerland the alps especially. Now I've toured Italy to Rome. I spent two days in Rome. I left now for Pisa. then the French Riviera. I've been on the move so much I've not written much to anyone. I bought a motor scooter. I've traveled ab… miles on it so … is great but …
Take Care

Mr Russel Foor
1838 6th STREET
ALTOONA

1. LODI
2. PIACENZA
3. FIDENZA
4. PARMA
5. REGGIO
6. MODENA
7. BOLOGNA
8. FORLI
9. RIMINI
10. PESARO
11. ANCONA

ALBERGO
RISTORANTE
BAR

Turismo

Imola
Via Emilia levante 45 . Tel. 2771
Ponte sul Santerno

N. 8902

Data

Signor

Pane e coperti	100	
Vino Minerale	150	
Antipasto		
Minestra		
Secondo e contorno	600	
Formagg.	180	
Dolce		
Frutta		
Caffè		
Servizio %	100	
	TOTALE L.	1130
Camera N. 15		1000
Bagno		2130
Garage		100
Servizio 15%		
Tassa soggiorno		
I.G.E. 2%		
	TOTALE L.	2230
Colazione del		
Consumazioni varie		
Telefono		
	IMPORTO TOTALE L.	

I.G.E. in abbonamento

PRINCIPAUTÉ
DE MONACO

GRANDE ALBERGO

IMPERATORE TRAIANO

☎ 945.307 - 945.308 - 945.99.22

GROTTAFERRATA

A 10 KM. DA ROMA

12 saloni per congressi e banchetti - riscaldamento ed aria condizionata - 300 posti letto. Tutti confort. Parcheggio per 500 autovetture.

12 halls for meetings and parties heating and air conditioning 300 beds. All confort. Parking for 500 cars.

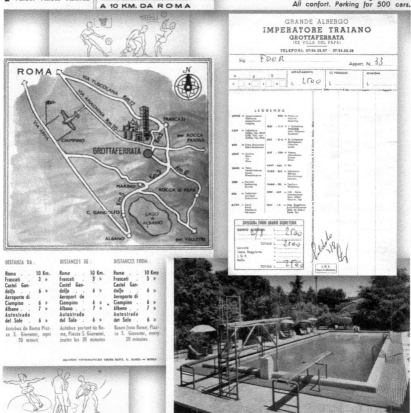

ROMA
VIA TUSCOLANA Km.12
VIA ANAGNINA Km.10
VIA APPIA
CIAMPINO
FRASCATI
per ROCCA PRIORA
GROTTAFERRATA
MARINO
ROCCA di PAPA
C. GANDOLFO
LAGO di ALBANO
ALBANO
per VELLETRI

DISTANZA DA:		DISTANCES DE:		DISTANCES FROM:	
Roma . .	10 Km.	Rome . .	10 Km.	Rome . .	10 Kms
Frascati .	3 »	Frascati .	3 »	Frascati .	3 »
Castel Gandolfo . .	6 »	Castel Gandolfo . .	6 »	Castel Gandolfo . .	6 »
Aeroporto di Ciampino .	6 »	Aeroport de Ciampino	6 »	Aeroporto di Ciampino .	6 »
Albano . .	7 »	Albano . .	7 »	Albano . .	7 »
Autostrada del Sole .	6 »	Autostrada del Sole .	6 »	Autostrada del Sole .	6 »

Autobus da Roma Piazza S. Giovanni, ogni 20 minuti

Autobus partant de Rome, Piazza S. Giovanni, toutes les 20 minutes

Buses from Rome, Piazza S. Giovanni, every 20 minutes

AZIENDE TIPOGRAFICHE EREDI DOTT. G. BARDI — ROMA

GRANDE ALBERGO
IMPERATORE TRAIANO
GROTTAFERRATA
(EX VILLA DEL PAPA)

TELEFONI: 07/94.53.07 - 07/94.53.08

Sig. FDOR Appart. N. 33

A	B	D	APPARTAMENTO	1/2 PENSIONE	PENSIONE
C ☐ S ☐ L ☐ D ☐			L. 2500	L.	L.

LEGGENDA

CHIUSURA FUORI ORARIO SEGRETERIA

CONTO ALBERGO 1/8 L. 2500

TOTALE L. 2500

Servizio
Tassa Soggiorno
I. G. E.
Bollo

TOTALE L. 2500

RISTORANTE La Perla

Propr. Bassi / Flüeler
Tel. 092 6 85 38

Data, 3/7.64
Camera N. 3

Nota per sig.

Camera	12	–
Colazione		
1 Day's taxe	–.	40
Bagno		
Telefono		
Diversi		
	12	40
Servizio 12 %	1	50
TOTALE	13	90

HOTEL VENDOME
MENTON

TÉL. 35-86-00
R. C. 60 A 154

Chambre No.

M Foor

Mois	5-8	6.8
Arrangements	25.00	25.00
Appartement		
Petit Déjeuner		
Lunch		
Diner		
Bières, Limonade, Eaux Miné.		
Bains		
Téléphone		
Divers		
Note du Jour	25.00	25.00
Report		25.00
TOTAL à reporter		50.00
Paiement		

Taxe de Séjour
Total Général

Hotel Tirrenus
PERUGIA
FRAZIONE MONTEBELLO
TEL. 70.818

Appart. N. 15

001185

Sig.

Mese Luglio 1964	1	2
Pensione - Arrangement - Pension		
Appartamento Chambre - Room - Zimmer	1700	
Riscaldamento Chauffage - Heating - Heizung		
Prima colazione Petit déjeuner-Breakfast-Frühstuck		200
Colazione Déjeuner - Lunch - Mittagessen		
Pranzo Diner - Dinner - Abendessen		
Extra		
Servizio in appartamento Service aux étages - Service in the Apartment		
Vini - Birra - Acque minerali Boissons - Drinks - Getränke		
Caffetteria - Bar		
Bagni - Bains - Baths - Bäder		
Biancheria Blanchissage - Washing - Wäsche		
Telefono		
Autobus e bagagli Bagages - Luggages - Gepäcke		
Autorimessa - Garage		
SOMMA DEL GIORNO Total du jour - Amount of day - Tagessumme		
Riporto - Vortrag		
TOTALE		
Pagamenti Encaissements - Settlements - Zahlungen		
Da riportare À reporter - Forward - Uebertrag		

I. G. E. IN ABBONAMENTO

Si prega di saldare il … giorno della …
On est prié … le jour de …
Bills are … presented …
Es wird … Rechnung am Abteilungstag zu begleichen.

Importo del conto Total - Amount - Summe
Rivalsa I.G.E. - Impôt
Servizio - Service
Imposta soggiorno Taxe séjour - Town tax
Bollo di quietanza
SOMMA DOVUTA À payer-Total amount

№ 2925

Albergo Hotel Pension
Rio - Lugano

Propr.: M. Kunz - Brügger
Via Cantonale 9 Tel. (091) 2 81 44 / 45

5 minute au dessous de la Gare
2 minute de la ville

Camera No. 16/21

Nota per il Sig.: Signori Wan Kirk - Foor Burrola

		Total
Déjeuner - Frühstück	4	
Chambre - Zimmer	4 à 13.50	
Souper - Nachtessen	mit Service und	
Diner - Mittagessen	Kurtaxe inbeg.	54.–
Pension	3 Briefchen	.70
Vin - Wein	Heizung	6.–
Bière - Bier		
Cigares		
Café - Thé		
Téléphone		
Kurtaxe		
Service		
Total		60.70

Lugano, il 7. 11. 64

Acquitée avec remerciement – Dankend empfangen

Chapter Six: Barcelona, Spain

On Sunday, August 9th, I arrived at what I thought was Paco's address. I drove around the place twice, not sure I was at the right residence. Where was the ocean Paco had bragged about being at his back door? And what about the fresh vegetable garden and chickens? Nothing here resembled what Paco had described. A six-foot-high, adobe-colored wall surrounded the property.

My face was dirty from traveling so closely behind diesel trucks across the flooded roads. I found a tree to put my right foot up to push the scooter back on its stand. I pulled my hair back under my head scarf and walked to a door in need of repair and paint. A short, Spanish woman appeared in a black dress with a hem down to the top of her shoes, a dark apron and a gray bandana around her head. A few wisps of white hair were visible surrounding her weather-beaten face. I inquired, "Is this Paco Hidalgo's residence?"

She looked up with a partial smile, *"Hola. Eres senorita Joan?"*

"Yes, si, si," I responded like an idiot. She looked over at my scooter with suitcases attached and made a motion for me to wait. She disappeared behind the wall. Looking inside the doorway, I could see a bit of what looked like a patio garden.

A few moments later, the woman came back with a short younger woman with dark hair and dark brown eyes resembling Paco. She greeted me like an old friend. "Welcome! *Como estas? Mi nombre es Pilar.* Come, come," she said, motioning with her arms to come inside the door. A few young chickens scattered across the ground in front of me. I saw a garden and smiled to myself.

I was beginning to understand Paco's explanation that his life here in San Adrian Del Besos ("The City of Kisses") was quite a distance from Barcelona. What a coincidence that Paco came from this city. His kisses were one of a kind and "special," I was certain of that. Lucky for me Paco's sister Pilar, Mario the brother-in-law, and the nephew spoke some English. His mother was difficult to even attempt to communicate with. I used my Spanish dictionary and spent an hour looking up word after word. Paco's family was wonderfully warm and friendly. They welcomed me to stay with his mother, but I insisted on them taking me to a nearby hotel. Paco's mother asked when Paco was planning on returning. I tried to convey that I wasn't sure. She handed me mail addressed to me that she had been holding.

I followed Pilar to a small, locally-owned hotel, Matacas, about three blocks away from Paco's house. The roads were not paved, but I could see the ocean, which was about the distance of a city block away. Now I experienced what Paco meant by breathing fresh air from the ocean. His home was close to the ocean, but I had pictured a large white ranch-styled house on the Spanish coast.

The staff at the hotel was friendly and accommodating. Pilar introduced me as the fiancée. Everyone was pleased to meet me and expressed how fond they were of Paco. The owner couldn't say enough about how great a soccer player he was.

I was escorted to a nice room; it was plain but adequate. They showed me where to park my scooter safely out of the weather. The restaurant in the hotel was huge. Pilar related something about tomorrow at lunchtime and left. I smiled and Juanita, a hotel worker, used my small dictionaries in French and Spanish to explain that the Hidalgo restaurant was within walking distance. She drew a little diagram on a small piece of paper with the address. I was to meet the family there around noon the next day.

I read my mail from Paco giving me strict instructions to stay with his mother. But there was no mention of how long I was to remain. I couldn't communicate with his mother making it impossible to stay with her. And there was no mention of a specific date for his arrival. Therefore, I would travel on and look for further mail as to when he planned to join me. Also there was good news from home, forwarded by Jan in Germany, sent from Aunt Anna and my brother. But the check I was expecting was not there. I had one more stock certificate I could sell for cash. My traveler's checks were down to a balance of only $120.00. I would have to head back to Germany to follow up on my vacation check which my brother would forward on to Jan.

What an interesting lunch with Pilar and her family. I met his brother who couldn't have been more cordial. He had me sampling different drinks at the bar. After I took a sip he would ask, "Do you have in America?" At least, I thought that was what he was asking in Spanish. When I was served clam shells and crawfish with their eyes staring up at me, I wasn't sure how my fork should tackle it. I watched his sister twirl with her small fork inside a shell removing the contents. Looking up with a smile, Pilar placed the mussel meat in her mouth and chewed it.

With the tiny fork I followed suit as though I had done it many times before. I didn't know what to expect but managed to get the contents from the mussel shell to my mouth. It was tough like gristle but surprisingly sweet in flavor. After devouring several mussels I acted like a pro. The crawfish was another matter. Pulling the meat out of the tail with a thin shell crackling turned me off. I did manage to save face and eat two forks full. Her brother served me a martini followed with champagne during the meal. Pilar served chicken with melon. The meal was deliciously exciting. I ate foods I had never eaten before. Afterwards I was poured a small crème de mint.

Everyone was anxious and somewhat confused trying to get some answers to their questions in broken English. I did my best to look up words to move the conversation along. You would have thought I was a blood relative receiving so much kindness and attention. Also, the family was interested to know all about America and how Paco was doing.

Senora Hidalgo sat quietly observing. She spoke a few words

quietly to the daughter every now and then. After several hours I heard her say, "*Vamos a mi casa.*"

Paco's brother replied, "*Si,si, madre vamos a,*" everyone looked in Senora Hidalgo's direction and began to straighten up the table.

Pilar said, "We go now," motioning for me to follow. Senora Hidalgo headed for the door with everyone in tow. They drove me back to Paco's house.

Hours slipped away at the Hidalgo home. His mother turned page by page through several albums of Paco's photographs. This was the first I saw his mother show joy, she smiled and laughed along with Spanish comments that I didn't understand. But her eyes and smiles revealed how much she loved Paco. His childhood and professional career meant everything to her. She kept a scrapbook with clippings during his career.

I found out Senora Hidalgo's house was the only one in the neighborhood having a walk-in shower. Broken English and looking up words with my dictionary, I gathered Paco had it shipped from America and installed for her. I left the house at seven o'clock that evening and walked back to my hotel. I went straight to bed. It was a wonderful, but trying day.

I lay in bed thinking of Paco and wishing he were here with me visiting his family. What a great opportunity to meet everyone. Each day in Spain brought me closer to understanding him. The question remained, Did I love him enough to want to spend my life in Spain? I'd been welcomed into the family without question. His mother thought it strange, my arriving via motor scooter. However, Pilar and Mario, her husband, told her my reason for traveling this way. After the explanations of cost were given, she looked over at me and smiled. Whether or not it was a smile of approval, I'm not entirely sure. She expressed through Pilar to me that Paco insisted I was to stay with her until he arrived. I nodded that I understood, but I knew it was not in my plan.

A week had passed, and my hair needed a touch up. The coiffeur charged only $2.12 for the works—bleached, washed and set.

On my way back to the hotel I stopped to visit awhile with

Pilar. Her smile and mannerisms were a constant reminder of Paco. She took me to her shoe store and insisted I pick out a pair of shoes. The Spanish sizes were different, and most shoes were too tight, uncomfortable, and very expensive. She insisted I take a pair. After trying on several styles I reluctantly agreed to take a pair of soft, blue, leather-soled bedroom slippers.

As usual, we communicated word-for-word from my dictionary. It was a laborious task, but I was beginning to learn some Spanish. She gave me a brown leather pair of men's shoes to deliver to Paco. They looked expensive. I didn't know how I was going to fit them into my suitcase. But I agreed to see he got them.

I took the shoes back to the hotel before taking the train into Barcelona. It was a short ride on an above-ground train. It reminded me of the one I used to ride from West Philadelphia to downtown Philly. The people bustling about reminded me of New York with all its crowds. Open fruit markets and cafés were lined up all along the street, and movie theatres were set back away from the sidewalks. Beloved American films such as *Can-Can* were showing. I chuckled to myself as I wandered in and out of a variety of different shops.

Walking farther down the street, a young man approached me from the side. "Do you speak English?" he asked. I put myself on guard, hesitating before responding with, "Yes."

He then said, "I'm from Turkey and here on holiday." His face lit up and was offered with a big grin. "Where are you from?" Although my ears perked up when I heard English spoken, I wasn't in the mood to encourage his tagging along.

"Excuse me! I'm going into this shop." I darted through the open doorway and lost him in the crowd of shoppers. I spent the rest of the afternoon browsing and enjoyed comparing the prices of clothing to those at home.

I rode the train back to the stop near my hotel, watching to ensure I didn't miss it. I freshened up, had a nice dinner, and went to bed.

The next day I slept in until ten o'clock in the morning. I thought, *I've been eating and sleeping too much lately. Soon they'll be saying* "Ella es demasiado gorda" (meaning, "She is too fat"). I asked Juanita where I could wash my dirty clothes. She escorted me to the roof of the hotel. There was a faucet over a sink that looked like the utility sink in my garage. Also, I noticed a medium-sized, wood-framed, corrugated metal washboard and a bar of brown soap. The soap made a lot of suds but burned the skin on my hands. My back was killing me after rubbing all my clothes and leaning over to rinse them. I hung them on a clothesline stretched across the roof of the hotel. I looked out from the roof to the ocean and across the dirt roads and small houses. It started to rain, so I grabbed my wet clothes, took them to my room, and hung them on hangers to dry. I wanted to go back to Barcelona, but the rain got too heavy. I was stuck and began thinking of traveling on in a couple of days.

On Thursday, August the 13th, I rode the train back to Barcelona. I didn't know why, but someone was always trying to tag along with me. A young, attractive, Spanish man with curly black hair by the name of Raphael began walking alongside me. He spoke rapid Spanish, from which I could only catch a familiar word now and then. He pulled at my arm, trying to lead me to a side street, pointing to his Vespa. He motioned that he wanted me to go for a ride. I shook my head, "No."

Raphael turned around and pointed to a café entrance. I was thirsty and followed him to a booth near the front door. We both ordered a Coca-Cola. After the waiter delivered our drinks, I turned toward him taking a sip of my coke. His dark eyes were devilish looking, and he was grinning from ear to ear. At the same time, he pointed to his male endowment that had somehow slipped out of the front of his trousers.

My smile turned into a frown of disgust. I grabbed my purse and ran out of the café as fast as I could. I turned down a one-way street, rounded another corner, and went down another street, periodically looking back over my shoulder. I was disappointed, shocked, and embarrassed. I walked off my frustration and dismay the rest of the day until my feet were killing me.

I returned to San Adrian del Besos at ten that night. I was wet from the rain and my hairdo was undone. My thoughts turned again to Paco's warning: "A woman should not travel alone in Europe." It was apparent he knew more about the Spanish male than I did.

Some German men were partying at my hotel and motioned for me to join their table. I responded with, "*Ich verstehen nicht.*" I thought that meant, "I don't understand." It worked regardless of whether I was correct or not. I had my dessert and left the restaurant.

Juanita said, "*Mucho bonita ropa*" ("So many nice clothes"). I laughed when she handed me a heavy iron to press my clothes on an old wobbly wooden ironing board. The iron was heavy like my grandmother's. It plugged in, but had no dial to regulate it. I feared it would burn holes in my clothes. Carefully I pressed my blouses and skirts.

I went back to Barcelona to get the pictures I left for developing. I had shots of the Hidalgo family and sites around the city. Most of them turned out despite the cloudy weather. The cost for developing was like that in America. I returned to the hotel and had dinner with cake and ice-dream for dessert. If it doesn't rain tomorrow I plan to travel on.

On Saturday, the 15th of August, I went to visit Pilar and Mario to say goodbye. Their home was small like a condo, situated on the fourth floor of a building. It felt warm and cozy. I met their children who were polite and friendly. Their youngest boy, Pedrito, was so cute. I invited them to visit California. What I gathered from their broken English was they were too old at 42. I relayed as best I could that they were still young and should travel to California. During the eight-hour visit, I ate delicious food, sharing again different drinks they wanted me to taste.

Meeting and visiting Paco's family was a highlight of my trip. I thanked Pilar and Mario for their hospitality and hoped they understood my English and sincerity. I hugged everyone goodbye. I could see the sadness in their eyes. I fought back tears of joy for all their kindness. I will always cherish this visit. No money could ever buy such an experience. At the same time, I wondered how and when we would meet again. Paco made no mention of the date of his arrival that I could share with his family. I will travel back to Germany looking for more mail from him. I was glad for my visit and wondered what the future will bring.

Chapter Seven: Spanish Coast

I packed my scooter and headed for Valencia, which was farther down the Spanish coast. Driving down the road, I reached an intersection where a traffic cop, dressed in a white uniform, was standing on a small, elevated platform. He was posted in the middle of several intersecting roadways. He motioned with his arm and his whistle for me to stop. I hit the brakes and landed on my stomach in the middle of the road. My scooter was on its side in the dirt, the wheels still spinning around.

The policeman came to my aid and helped me to my feet. My pant leg was torn where my leg was bleeding. I was bruised with brush burns on my arm and hand. I limped over to my Heinkel. The policeman helped me get it upright. I checked it over and found a small dent in the transmission, but it had no apparent leaks. My suitcases had many scrapes and scratches.

When the officer had ordered me to stop, my wheels must have slid due to fine sand on the road. I don't know how I lost my grip and flew over the handlebar.

After remounting the scooter, I was able to drive onward, but I was on edge and sick to my stomach. I stopped earlier than usual at a nice hotel. I was worried about my abdomen soreness and being sick to my stomach.

At dinner I only had soup with a glass of wine which I hoped would make me feel better. The alcohol made me sleepy and I went to bed early.

On Monday, August 17th, I stopped to take a picture of a

waterwheel on my day's journey. Farther down the road a man waved me down saying, *"Maletas,"* and pointing to my suitcases. I got it! My two suitcases on the back rack were about to fall from my scooter. I repositioned them and fastened the elastic ropes tighter.

"Thank you. *Gracias*," I said with a smile.

"Mi nombre es Perlito," he responded pointing to a weird-looking restaurant. He looked typically Spanish with the dark hair, medium build and terrific teeth which sparkled when he smiled. I removed my large purse from the scooter and followed him. He parted the long beads hanging across the doorway for me to enter. It was dark inside and reminded of a foreign film I saw years ago but couldn't remember its title.

I ordered a beer, took out my two translation dictionaries and we began to try to communicate. An hour passed and I realized it was almost time for me to stop for the night.

"Hoy algún hotel cerca?" I wasn't sure of the pronunciation, but I tried.

He smiled and replied, *"Pente muy bonita."* I gathered his message meant there was a nice hotel nearby. *"Muy poco dinero."* I understood "poco" and "dinero," meaning it must not cost much.

I followed his Fiat down the road. He pulled into a vacant area alongside a strange-looking, two-story building. I followed but then hesitated; it didn't look like a hotel. I went inside and asked, "Do you have running water?"

"Si, si, Senorita," which I understood as a "Yes." When the manager took me upstairs to my room, all I saw was a large beige pitcher of water beside a wooden stand with a porcelain bowl in the center. A large cork was stuck in the middle of the bowl as a stopper. There was a dim ceiling light coming from a white glass fixture. It was probably dim on purpose so you didn't notice the old bed that swayed in the center due to worn-out metal springs.

I wasn't happy with the accommodations, but it was too late to try to find another place. I needed to find a restroom fast. I was feeling extreme pressure from my bladder. The words I spoke were *toilette, bano, necessario,* bathroom—and *caca* as a last resort, thinking it meant "shit." The owner didn't get it. I was desperate and started to loosen the buttons at the top of my slacks. I bent down like I was going to let my urine drop.

"Si, si, Senorita," the young man said. He led me out the backdoor to an outhouse. This was an outside toilet I would rather not have found except for my need right then. Two round holes were in an old wooden board covered with aluminum pot lids. I lifted a lid and, in a half-standing position, relieved my bladder. This was a poor excuse for an outhouse. It was worse than any I had experienced—nothing like the one Dad built and we used for years at our cottage along the river. I went back to my scooter, unloaded my bags, and went reluctantly up to my room.

It was after dark when Perlito came asking for me. He invited me to the cinema. The movie playing was old, with Anne Baxter and Rock Hudson, dubbed in Spanish. We walked through the entrance which led back outside to benches under the stars. It was like a drive-in movie, but you walked in. Perlito gave comments in Spanish, which I rarely understood. I followed as he escorted me back to this weird hotel where he wanted me to stay the next day. I bid him a goodnight and went to my room. My bed sheets looked like they had just been slept in. The pillowcase actually had red lipstick marks on it. I placed what appeared to be an unused towel over the marks and fell into the squeaky sunken-in mattress.

I fell off to sleep. When I awoke, I rushed to pack and check out. The biggest kick out of the whole experience was the cost. I figured it out to be equivalent to forty-two cents a day in American money. A bargain for sure, but I certainly wouldn't recommend it!

The following morning I searched for a repair shop to get an oil change. I couldn't get the man to understand my broken Spanish from my dictionary. I took hold of his hand and led him to my scooter and pointed to the housing that holds the oil. Everyone laughed at my demonstration, but I didn't think it was one bit funny.

Afterward, I followed the coastline. The weather was warm

and dry like Palm Springs, California. The sand was clean and bright, almost white. It reminded me of Manhattan Beach—that is, without any expensive homes overlooking the ocean. The dark blue ocean waves with white caps were breaking and slapping against the sandy beach. Farther back from the ocean were some large estates painted white that did have a coastal view.

Southern Spain is a beautiful area with the friendliest people. It's hard to say, but I believe friendlier than any of the countries I'd toured so far. Everyone waved to me as I drove down the road, whether it was a man on a cart pulled by a donkey, or a woman working along the highway. Some of the men removed their sombreros as I passed by. These gestures were so welcoming. I felt like a movie star passing through. I couldn't feel more carefree than I did at that moment. I would treat myself that night to a modern hotel overlooking the ocean.

When I located my place for the night, I discovered that my accommodations were great and included an adjoining bath. I enjoyed having a delicious dinner and living like I had arrived by a Mercedes car or a limo. The other guests dining around me would never have guessed I was the girl they'd seen earlier on the motor scooter. I looked out my window and a full golden moon hung over a dark blue calm ocean below. I hated to move on because the place reminded me of Miami Beach, Florida.

I had only gone a short distance the next day when my scooter started backfiring and my engine sputtered. I pulled into a garage with a loud bang! This time they heard me coming. It wouldn't be a mystery as to what needed to be done. A young bullfighter by the name of Pepe showed me his poster with second billing on the wall. He was lean, short, and attractive, fitting the bill for the bullfighters I had seen in Tijuana, Mexico years before. Obviously, he was also a mechanic and worked on my engine. The cost was thirty-five pesetas, and my scooter checked out okay.

I drove farther along the coast, stopping at several places, and couldn't find any vacancies. I stopped for a drink in a restaurant/bar that looked a lot like an American motel. I drank a coke and spoke with Michele, the female bartender, who was from Canada.

"I can't find a vacancy this evening along the coast. Do you know of anywhere I can find a room near here for the night?" I inquired.

She replied, "I don't think my husband will mind if I rent out his studio upstairs; it does have a bathroom and shower. He isn't using it at present." I followed her up the steps, and the room was delightful.

"Go ahead and take your baggage upstairs; it will be all right," she offered.

I thought, *What if her husband objects?* But I started lugging my suitcases through the bar and upstairs to the studio. On my second trip past the bar to the stairs, Michele yelled over to me, "Come down and have dinner with us. I want my husband and friends to meet you."

"Thanks, I'll be down after I shower!" I replied. I was delighted to speak English for the evening. I met her husband and three friends from London. We ate, had a few drinks, and told jokes for hours. When her husband found out I was the woman on the blue motor scooter he'd passed on the road earlier, he was shocked.

"You are a brave woman traveling like that," he said. Everyone lifted their glasses and made a toast to me. I guess one could say I was rather brave.

Chapter Eight: Gibraltar & North Africa (The Casbah)

On August 20th, Thursday, I arrived in Gibraltar. Only one double room was available; $9.00 per night, paid in English pounds. This was the most spacious room I'd had thus far. Another surprise was that the hot water was hot, not lukewarm like most.

Later I decided to try kidney pie. It was interestingly English.

The next morning I ventured out without baggage. I visited St. Michael's Cave and Europa Point, where the apes lived with their little babies. It was a cloudy day with a fine mist, making it difficult to get a good Brownie movie shot. Handling my scooter around the hills without luggage was fun. After returning to my hotel, I took a hot shower and washed my hair. This was the first hot water since my night outside of Monaco.

I tried another English meal of kidneys that evening; not bad. Everyone there spoke English, which was a pleasant change. The next day, I would head for Tangiers, North Africa.

I started my day with a regular English breakfast with eggs and bacon—my first real English style breakfast since New York.

I missed the ferry across to Tangiers because they stopped selling tickets earlier; the hotel had misinformed me. Rather than wait I decided to take a ferry to Algerceras, Spain. The lines going through customs were crowded with people pushing from line to line to get a ticket. I met a young man who spoke English; Luciano was from Casa Blanca. He had dark skin, black hair slicked back from his forehead, and dark brown devilish eyes. He boasted of being able to speak five different languages. I had a pounding headache and regretted wasting three hours trying to get aboard the ferry that ran straight to Tangiers. Luciano invited me to the café for a Cuba Libra drink made with tea. The ferry was rocky due to a rough sea which made me seasick. Luciano visited with me the entire trip. He explained, "I would drive you onto shore, but it is too dangerous." My scooter was on a lower level than his car. I didn't understand why he would think I would want to ride off the ferry with him.

"What are you saying? I need to drive my scooter onto shore," I explained.

"That's right, I forgot," he replied. "Well, you see, I've expensive oriental rugs hidden in my trunk. I purchased them and don't want to pay customs. If they catch me, I will be in trouble and detained. I don't want to involve you. I'll watch for your scooter once I'm through the check point."

"Thanks for letting me know what you are up to," I said.

"When you see my car drive off the ferry, follow me. I will lead you into the city of Tangiers. I used to live there and love it. Let me show you around and take you to the Casbah."

"I appreciate your leading me into Tangiers," I replied. He had pointed out his gray Mercedes earlier.

"Okay, I'll look for your car coming from the ferry and through customs."

I thought, *This guy is headed for trouble and I don't want to be any part of it.* Once his Mercedes drove off the ferry, I maneuvered to get behind him. Following his car into the city made it easy for me. He parked alongside a hotel and I pulled up behind him.

"I want to take you in here for lunch. It's an old familiar place. Your scooter and your belongings are safe here. Don't worry!" he insisted.

Reluctantly, I removed my purse and followed him into a beautiful hotel restaurant. The waiters were dressed in Moroccan festive outfits with beige trousers that bloused to below the knee and bright red fez hats with tassels. The walls were a dark red with large bright golden tapestries hanging from the ceiling to floor at the windows. Luciano ordered some fancy sandwiches. First the waiter brought two Cuba Libras. Hot tea came later served out of a large silver tea pot.

"Joan, let me further explain about my business here. I transport rugs from Europe to Casa Blanca. I know it's risky to try to slip through customs but paying tax between countries means no profit. This is the only way I can make money."

"I understand, but what if you get caught?"

"So far, I've been lucky, and I love coming back to Morocco frequently."

From the hotel he drove me to the private Italian school he had attended when young. The mosaics and wood carvings were done by hand hundreds of years ago. The building was full of old art and beautifully decorated. We headed for the Casbah and spent the afternoon going through the museum, visiting the old king's casa, and walking up and down narrow passageways. There were vendors sitting along the paths with old rusty locks and hardware laid out in front of them for sale. Other small shops had belts, handbags, and decorative beads for sale. Luciano pointed to a multicolored shear silk scarf and said, "Let me purchase this for you."

I immediately refused, "No, thank you. But I would like a picture of me standing here in the Casbah."

"Let me hold onto your purse," he said. He hung my purse handles over his forearm while I unzipped the bottom removing my camera and handed it to him. He took off running with my camera and purse hanging on his arm up the hill. Suddenly I panicked, realizing he had run off with my critical possessions. I started running up the hill after him as fast as I could. When I reached him at the top of the hill I was out of breath. He looked startled and surprised, "I thought you wanted me to get your picture from up here?"

"I did, I mean I do, but…" I didn't know what to say. I could barely speak. I thought he was running away with all my possessions. I realized he was innocent at this point. What a relief after a frightening few minutes.

The rest of the afternoon was interesting and exciting. To think I was really here on the narrow streets of the Casbah. My brother had sent me pictures from when he visited years before that interested me. It was getting late and time to find a hotel for the night.

"Joan, why not spend a few more days here?" he asked. "We can drive to Casa Blanca and I can show you more of Morocco?"

"No, I really can't stay," I replied. "I need to head up toward Portugal. I promised my brother I would come to Morocco to see the country where he was stationed when in the Air Force. I hadn't planned on spending more than a day here."

It was tempting to go on to Casa Blanca. The farther I went, the more I wanted to see.

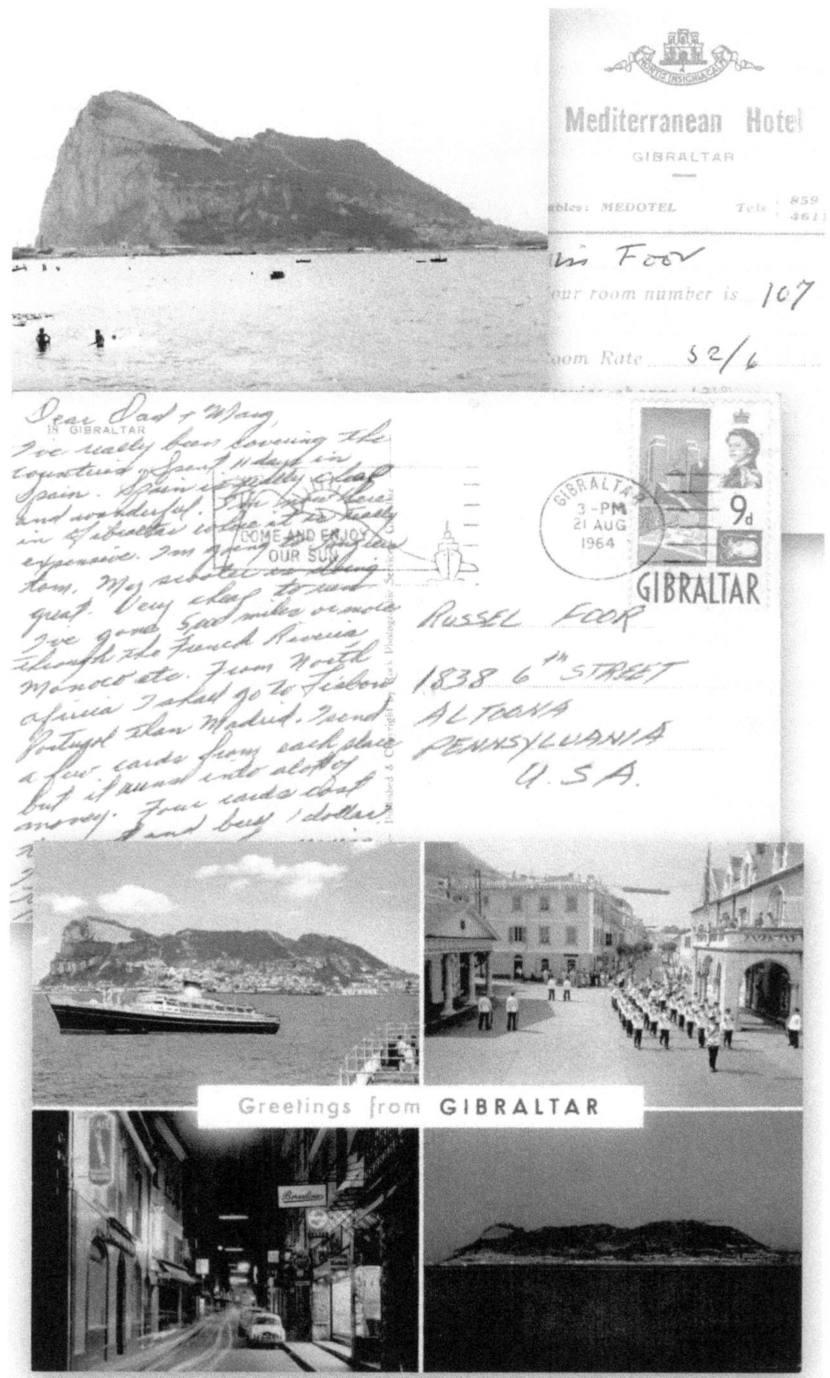

Mediterranean Hotel
GIBRALTAR
Cables: MEDOTEL
Tels 859 4611
Foor
Your room number is 107
Room Rate 52/6
Dear Dad & Mary
18 GIBRALTAR
COME AND ENJOY OUR SUN
GIBRALTAR 3-PM 21 AUG 1964
9d
GIBRALTAR
RUSSEL FOOR
1838 6th STREET
ALTOONA
PENNSYLVANIA
U.S.A.
Greetings from GIBRALTAR

Man tried to break in =
Nº 000290
Hostal Km. 113
RESTAURANTE - BAR
ALGORA (Guadalajara)
Teléfono núm. 2
MESA n.º
N.º
CONCEPTO
PESETAS
habitacion 9
70
29
99
Restaurante MATACAS
Avda. Eduardo Maristany, núm. 21 - Teléfono 66
San Adrián de Besós, 16 de Agosto de 196
PESETAS
1050
Calzados "RIVERO"
Señora - Caballero y Niño
Avenida del Caudillo, 43 - Teléfono 309
San Adrián del Besós
P'a que después digan que uno no da buenos tropezones
5 PTAS MADRID
ESPAÑA
CORREOS
02232
BARCELONA - TERMINO
BADALONA
IDA
VUELTA
BADALONA
BARCELONA - TERMINO
3ª CLASE
PTS 6
T.E. 2-A II.
02232
Los Faroles
BAR - BUNGALOWS - PLAYA
MARBELLA (Km. 182) Río Verde
(MÁLAGA)
Spain

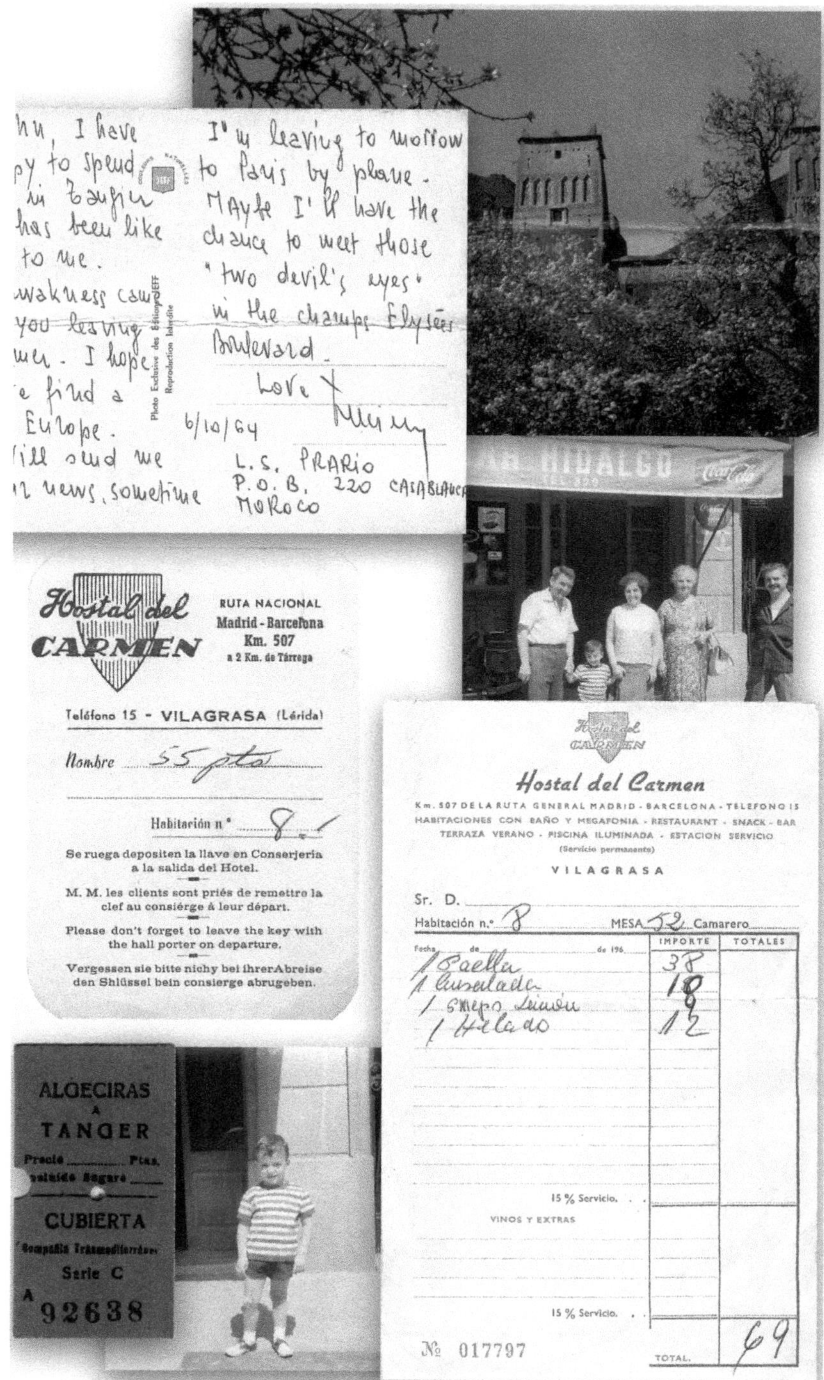

...hn, I have ...py to spend ... in Tangier ... has been like ... to me. ...wakness came ... you leaving ... when. I hope ...e find a ... Europe. ...ill send me ...r news, sometime

I'm leaving tomorrow to Paris by plane. Maybe I'll have the chance to meet those "two devil's eyes" in the champs Elysées Boulevard.

Love X

6/10/64

L.S. PRARIO
P.O.B. 220 CASABLANC...
MOROCO

Photo Exclusive des Editions JEFF
Reproduction Interdite

Hostal del CARMEN

RUTA NACIONAL
Madrid - Barcelona
Km. 507
a 2 Km. de Tárrega

Teléfono 15 - VILAGRASA (Lérida)

Nombre 55 ptas

Habitación n.º 8

Se ruega depositen la llave en Conserjería a la salida del Hotel.

M. M. les clients sont priés de remettre la clef au consiérge à leur départ.

Please don't forget to leave the key with the hall porter on departure.

Vergessen sie bitte nichy bei ihrerAbreise den Shlüssel bein consierge abrugeben.

Hostal del CARMEN

Hostal del Carmen

Km. 507 DE LA RUTA GENERAL MADRID - BARCELONA - TELEFONO 15
HABITACIONES CON BAÑO Y MEGAFONIA - RESTAURANT - SNACK - BAR
TERRAZA VERANO - PISCINA ILUMINADA - ESTACION SERVICIO
(Servicio permanente)

VILAGRASA

Sr. D.

Habitación n.º 8 MESA 52 Camarero

Fecha de de 196	IMPORTE	TOTALES
1 Paella	38	
1 Ensalada	10	
1 ...	9	
1 Helado	12	
15 % Servicio.		
VINOS Y EXTRAS		
15 % Servicio.		
№ 017797 TOTAL.		69

ALGECIRAS
A
TANGER
Precio ... Ptas.
...
CUBIERTA
Compañía Trasmediterránea
Serie C
A 92638

AFTER FIVE DAYS, RETURN TO
Francisco Hidalgo
1527 West 7th Street
Los Angeles (17) Calif.
U.S.A.
LOS ANGELES CALIF.
AM
15 AUG
1964
LIBERTY FOR ALL
US AIR MAIL 15
VIA AIR MAIL
Miss.
Joan Coll
C/ Santa Catalina Io
San Adrián del Besós
BARCELONA
ESPAÑA.
Avión
ESPAÑA
5 PTAS MURCIA
BARCELONA
Srta.
Joan L. Foor
c/o Sams T. Nelson
American International Underwriters
G.M.B.H.
Bahnhofstrasse 52
Wiesbaden 62 (ALEMANIA)
CAPERUCITA ROJA
¡Ayúdame Corderito!
dice la Caperucita
que aquel lobo tan malito
quiere atrapar a Abuelita.
Calzados "RIVERO"
Señora - Caballero y Niño
Avenida del Caudillo, 43 - Teléfono 309
San Adrián del Besós
"LOS FAROLES"
RIO VERDE - MARBELLA
SPAIN
Hidalgo

MEDITERRANEAN HOTEL

GIBRALTAR

INVOICE № 001387

Mr. Foor 22 - 8 - 1964

BILLS PAYABLE WHEN PRESENTED

ROOM No. 107	20/8	21/8	22/8
Brought forward		3 12 6	6 11 0
Apartments 1X52/6	2 12 6	2 12 6	
En pension			
Breakfast		6 0	
Luncheons			
Dinners	14 0		
Wines, Spirits	6 0		
Beers, Minerals			
Lounge: Drinks			
Lounge: Cons Coffee			
Lounge: Tea			
Bar			
Laundry			
Telephone			
Garage			
Transport			
Tobacco			
Room Service			
Cash			
Sundries			
TOTAL			6 11 0
Service & House Charge 12½%			16 6
TOTAL			7 7 6
Cash Received			
Carried Forward	3 12 6	6 11 0	

PLEASE LEAVE KEY BEFORE D

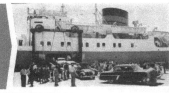

Bland Line

GIBRALTAR - TANGIER SERVICE

M. V. MONS CALPE

NORMAL SERVICES 1964

Daily (Sundays excepted) *All times local.*

Depart Gibraltar **1030 hours.**

Depart Tangier **1330 hours.**

SEASONAL SERVICES

From 26th June to 15th August (Except Sundays)

Depart Tangier 07.30 and 15.00 hours

Depart Gibraltar 12.00 and 19.30 hours

(N.B. The 19.30 hrs. Service on 15th August will not operate).

From 17th August to 3rd October (Except Sundays)

Depart Gibraltar 09.30 and 17.00 hours

Depart Tangier 12.00 and 19.30 hours

SPECIAL SUNDAY SERVICES

28th June and 5th July

Depart Tangier 07.30 and 15.00 hours

Depart Gibraltar 12.00 and 19.30 hours

12th, 19th and 26th July, 2nd, 9th August

Depart Tangier 07.30 hours

Depart Gibraltar 19.30 hours

16th, 23rd, 30th August and 6th & 13th September

Depart Gibraltar 09.30 hours

Depart Tangier 12.00 hours

20th and 27th September

Depart Gibraltar 09.30 and 17.00 hours

Depart Tangier 12.00 and 19.30 hours

NO SERVICE PERIODS

Good Friday—27th March.

Annual Overhauls—26th to 29th May, 3rd to 13th November

Christmas Day—25th December.

Local Times: Tangier=G.M.T. Gibraltar=G.M.T. plus 1 hour.

GIBRALTAR 21 AUG 1964

9d

GIBRALTAR

MRS ANNA LONBERGER

2652 NEWELL ST.

LOS ANGELES 39,

CALIFORNIA

U.S.A.

GIBRALTAR

No. 2039

HOTEL · GIBRALTAR

22 - 8 - 1964

pounds seven

pence in settlement / on account of

Mediterranean Hotel

Chapter Nine: Bound for Portugal

August 22nd, Saturday, I didn't get far before I ran out of gas again. I had to push the scooter along the road an equivalent to several city blocks in America. I guess I hadn't noticed the reserve tank light was on. After filling up the tank, I drove over 350 kilometers. I was near the Portugal border when it got dark and cold. I came across a small place with rooms for rent. I hated to stop, but getting stuck in the dark was dangerous.

At daybreak I drove on into Sevilla, Spain. Long, beautiful streets accommodated horse carriages, palm trees, and large villas. This was quite a contrast from where I had been along the coast of Malaga. What a clean-looking, interesting city. When I stopped for lunch, the bartender saw I had an American silver dollar. I wanted to exchange money for Spanish currency. He asked if he could give me sixty pesetas for it; I agreed.

I headed farther toward the Portugal border. I had to board another ferry to get to Lisbon. When I attempted to push my scooter on board, the front wheel got stuck between the wooden floorboards. I was struggling to push it forward.

"Wait a minute, I'll help you," offered a short, redheaded, young gentleman. He walked over, smiled, and shoved my wheel free.

"Where did you get this scooter?" he asked in English. I returned the smile, not only because he helped me, but hearing good English was always refreshing.

"I bought it in Frankfurt, Germany," I replied proudly.

"And you have driven it this far?" he asked.

"Yes, it's been quite a trip," I answered.

He introduced himself as Fernando. He had a bushy, full head of curly, red hair, freckles, and a pleasing smile. We were about the same height, and he had a strong, hefty-looking build. We walked together upstairs into the restaurant. Fernando introduced me to his father, Charles, and his uncle. From the top deck, Fernando pointed to his transportation, parked below. It was a Heinkel identical to mine, except in white.

"I can't believe you have the same scooter. Where did you get yours?" I asked.

"Heinkel scooters are sold here in Portugal. You will see many more in Lisbon. They perform well and get us back and forth to work," he added.

We had lunch together, talked about where I was from as well as where I was headed. He was interesting, and he explained that he was applying to be on an immigration quota to Canada.

"Wait until I get my Heinkel on land, and you can follow me through the city of Lisbon." He assisted me again by pushing my scooter off the ferry. I waited for him to get on his scooter once he exited the ferry. He pulled over in front of me. It was fun riding in tandem, two identical scooters, driving through the streets of such a busy large city. I stayed close behind. I didn't have a clue as to where I was going to stay in Lisbon. Fernando led me to St. George's Castle on our way to the university, Pensao Universitaria. He parked by the university dorms.

"I know the manager here. It's reasonable to stay during the summer, for the dorms are empty," he added. Fernando introduced me to the manager who advised me that the cost was twenty-eight escudo per day, which included breakfast. They showed me a large room with a private shower—and it was spotless. I had to agree to stay a minimum of four days.

"No problem, I can stay at least four days," I replied. "And what does that amount to in American money?" I asked.

"Well, that's about one dollar a day in American money."

"I believe I can afford that without a problem." The manager laughed wholeheartedly at my response. Fernando helped with carrying my luggage to the second floor.

"There is a fair in the city, and I would like to take you there. You can ride with me on my scooter," Fernando explained. This was a first! I climbed aboard his Heinkel as a passenger. He placed a small blanket over my legs before we drove off. It was a different experience, riding through the city from the back of the seat, holding onto his waist. At the fair, he ordered us delicious, fresh fruit drinks.

"Promise me you will stay more than four days. I want to show you Portugal," he said with a serious tone.

Fernando worked as a baker and was considered a skilled worker. Portugal put his name on a long list, making it extremely difficult to leave his country and migrate to Canada. Fernando was not pushy, nor did he make any flirtatious gestures toward me—at least not yet.

The turn signals on my scooter had stopped working. Fernando took my scooter that evening to fix my turn signals. I felt insecure with his taking my scooter, but I thought his familiarity with the university would make it okay. I was relieved the next morning to see my scooter and the lights working.

Portugal is very hilly and beautifully bright with a constant ocean breeze. I met Fernando at his large, modern bake shop. He took me to lunch nearby. Afterward I followed his scooter to the university gardens. We walked through, observing the statues at the university before returning to my dorm.

At eight that evening, he came by to take me on a tour of Lisbon at night. Once again, I rode in a skirt with my legs dangling like a saddle bag but from my own scooter. I think he got a kick out of covering my bare legs with a blanket.

I saw Lisbon at its finest—the historic monuments, the main hospital, and the small villages outside the city. At our last stop my scooter wouldn't start; the battery was dead. I got off my seat. Fernando ran alongside the scooter downhill, jumped on and caught it in gear. He turned around and came back to pick me up. He had fun showing me his city. I was enjoying the sightseeing and his companionship.

We arrived back at the dorm and he said, "I want you forever; I believe I love you."

"No," I replied, "you may think that, but you barely know me. It's the summer weather. And I'm a blonde from America whom you've met. However, this blonde is just traveling through. I'm promised to another man from Barcelona. I've just come from meeting his family."

"Please promise me you will stay until Monday," he asked politely.

"I will give it serious thought. Lisbon is a lovely city with much to see. I'm enjoying it and appreciate your showing me around."

I stayed on until Tuesday. Fernando met me at the dorm every morning before work for a continental breakfast with hot chocolate, fresh rolls, and marmalade. I was miserable with constipation, but I met Fernando for lunch as planned. When I returned to the dorm, the maid introduced me to an entertainer who rode a motorcycle around a large, barrel-shaped arena. He had seen me coming and going on my motor scooter.

"I can train you to ride in a circle just like I do. It will only take me about a month to teach you how. I can pay you two hundred American dollars per week." His name was Fernando too. I was flabbergasted. I could not picture myself riding a motorcycle around a track as an entertainer. I told him I really had no desire to be in that type of work. I agreed to meet him for lunch the next day to discuss it further.

I met the entertainer the next day and he led me to the round, wooden arena where he rode in a circle. It was like a racetrack, but he rode around the sides of this bowl. It was interesting, but certainly not something I wanted to learn to do. On the other hand, the money would be good.

Fernando the baker met me for dinner and insisted on my staying through the weekend. It was so difficult listening to him talk about his desire to have me stay in Portugal. He expressed again his love for me.

"Oh my, how do I get through to you that I can't accept your affection?" I asked. "I'm in love with another man. Don't you see this one-sided arrangement cannot work? I can't kiss you or be in any way affectionate toward you. I like you as a friend and nothing more."

"It doesn't matter. Please stay three more days for my sake," he pleaded. Perhaps, he thought a few more days would change my mind. He had been so kind and sweet; I felt sorry for him.

On Wednesday, Fernando introduced me to his best friend, Mario. Fernando promised, "He will take you sightseeing, for I have to work. I want you to see more of Portugal." I was skeptical but trusted Fernando's wanting me to see more of the city that he was so proud of.

Mario and I left Fernando and walked to the bus line. Mario took me to the top of Green Mountain. We saw the city from its highest point. He told me *Lisboa* means the "City of Seven Mountains." It was fun riding double decker buses, sitting on top, which was open like a convertible with the top down. I got a penetrating headache from the sun. We rode the subway back which was only a couple years old. I remarked how clean the city streets were. Mario told me the government of the republic was not good, and the people hated their government. I saw a lot of police officers with machine guns hanging from their shoulders on street corners and sitting in front of public buildings. To my knowledge, Portugal was a dictatorship and had been for years.

Fernando came by the dorm later. We talked about my staying through the weekend. I felt it was time to move on.

"Joan, listen, I want you to have a baby by me, then you would have to marry me. If you had my baby, you would love me," he added.

"Fernando, please get this notion out of your head," I insisted. "I'm not going to have your baby, and like I've told you before, I'm in love with someone else. You are a sincere and kind man. One day you will meet a girl who can reciprocate this love you think you have for me. Trust me! I'm not that girl."

On Thursday morning, at half past seven, I received a rap on my dorm door. Fernando stopped by for breakfast as usual.

"Mario will accompany you to the beach today. I wish I could go with you both. Have a good day. He will meet you up at the station," Fernando explained.

"Thanks for setting this up for me, Fernando. I hope your day isn't too busy." I packed a small bag with a towel and wore my bathing suit under my clothes. I met Mario at the train station. I enjoyed the scenery on our short train ride.

The beach here was different than the beaches in California. Small tents and cabanas of all colors were scattered along the coast. It was hot, and Mario rented a small tent to shield the sun. This was a new welcomed experience because the sun was unbearably hot. The ocean was calm, dark blue, leading to almost black in the distance due to the depth. I removed my street clothes, revealing my two-piece light-blue bathing suit, and we headed for the water. I dove in and Mario followed close behind. It was refreshing. We took a short swim out from the shore. It didn't take much until I was winded. I walked along the wet sand then made a quick run for the tent, trying to avoid burning my feet on the hot sand.

I patted dry and was positioning my towel to lie down. Without warning, Mario grabbed me around the waist from behind. As I turned my head, he kissed me passionately. I resisted, pushing him backward. He lost his balance and almost fell, but it didn't seem to matter. He remained calm and continued to talk about this being his favorite beach. I thought, *He had some nerve! Fernando is his best friend too, but that was quite a kiss he planted on me!* I didn't know what to say. So, I began to change the atmosphere and talked about meeting my new mother-in-law in Barcelona. Mario continued to joke around. He acted playful and calm as we made frequent visits to the ocean and back. He patted my leg occasionally while making a point, and he served me the lunch he brought along. I was on guard the rest of the day. He made no other advances, and I was glad.

Mario and I arrived late back at the dorm. Fernando was sitting on the edge of my bed and didn't seem happy with either of us. If only Fernando knew how Mario had behaved; he would be more than upset. Fernando was kind and always respected my wishes. It was difficult for him to keep from trying to make advances. He wanted to show me Portugal and I did let him hold my hand crossing the street—but that was it! Mario left and Fernando asked me to join him for dinner again.

"Please reconsider staying for the weekend. I want to spend more time with you. Give me a chance to express how much I love you," he said as our eyes met. He was so innocent and sweet, but his feelings were misplaced. I could not have been more honest; romance stood no chance between the two of us.

"No, Fernando. I'm sorry, but I can't stay longer," I answered. "You are a great guy and have been such a good friend. I've enjoyed seeing your city, thanks to you. I wish it could be different, but, in all honesty, it can't be." At that moment, I thought, *It will be best if I leave tomorrow morning without saying goodbye. I hate to run away, but it's better for him.*

On Friday, August 28th, I washed my clothes and started to pack to take off the next day. The maid and I talked a long while about Fernando. I explained to her how I wished things could have been different, but I was promised to another man.

Fernando showed up early evening and took me to dinner and a movie. It was an old movie with Rhonda Fleming and Bob Hope with dubbed-in English.

"I'll drive your scooter home tonight to check it out before your trip," Fernando said, determined.

"What if I want to go shopping tomorrow?" I asked. I thought, *Now I won't be able to sneak away without saying goodbye.*

"That's no problem. I will come at two o'clock tomorrow afternoon and take you anywhere you want to go," he responded quickly. I began to get concerned, for he was trying to get me to stay the weekend. He was so blinded by his affection for me. I could calm him down, but he was nervous and persistent. I worried about his behavior when I would try to leave. He wanted me to stay and become a citizen of Portugal. That would never happen. Now he had managed to manipulate me by taking away my scooter.

The next morning, I tagged along with Cecilia, the maid, downtown by metro. Cecilia pointed out different shops that had reasonable prices. I bought a blouse and headband. It was an education on finance to figure out the exchange rate of how much everything cost in American money. Cecilia gave me directions on getting back to the university and we parted. I continued to walk in and out of different shops for an hour or more. When I approached a large intersection, I saw a medium-sized group of people gathered on the corner. Being curious, I pushed my way through to the street. There were several policemen with machine guns walking down the street toward the crowd. Suddenly, a large hand covered my mouth and I was grabbed around the waist and led backward, away from the crowd.

"Be quiet. Don't make a sound," was whispered into my ear in English. I struggled to free myself from the firm grip of a hand across my face. When I was away from most of the people, my mouth was freed. I turned to face a middle-aged man.

"What's going on? Who are you?" I asked. I was frightened and upset at the same time.

"I apologize for being so rough, but you were in danger," he replied. "I watched you approaching those protestors and figured you were an American tourist who didn't know what was about to happen."

"I don't understand. What are you talking about?" I asked.

"Well, when our people protest, the police sometimes open fire into the crowd. They kill innocent bystanders like you. These protests many times get out of control. Most citizens do not like the dictatorship that rules here. Different groups opposing the government retaliate and blowup public buildings and form riots in the streets. The police take the upper hand," he said.

"A 'thank you' is in order then. I had no idea what was happening and never dreamed the police would fire real bullets into a crowd," I admitted. "After all of that, I've had enough excitement for today and will head back to my hotel."

"Be careful, and I'm sorry I scared you so. Good luck in your travels from here." He smiled. I returned the smile and walked toward the train.

When I arrived back at the university, Fernando was driving

my scooter up the road. He helped me get situated side saddle across the back seat. Fernando placed a shawl over my legs and drove me on my scooter to Mafra. We went through the museum and a convent that had the first Bible edition in several languages. The Kings Chamber and game room were impressive. We stopped at Height Palace. I climbed the spiral steps to the top. He drove me past two beaches, but we didn't stop. The scenery was beautiful.

Fernando took me to dinner; I didn't mention the incident down in the city. He bought tickets for the movie *Viva Las Vegas.* I had seen this film before. I found it boring. I thought to myself, *Tomorrow should be my last day in Portugal, but it wasn't to be.*

It was early when Fernando arrived. We had breakfast together as usual. I rode on his scooter toward Santa Cruz Beach. He stopped for me to view the Church of the Miracle. Farther down the road we came to acres of grape vineyards. Fernando pulled over and we walked into a vineyard; he picked two large bunches of grapes.

"By the way, this is against the law," he added. Worried, I looked all around and was relieved to see nothing but acres of vineyards. He laughed, "Don't worry; the farmers wouldn't care about our helping ourselves to so few."

It was a beautiful day at the beach. The sky was clear and not as hot as the day I had spent with Mario. Fernando spread out a large blanket on the sand. We sat watching people snorkeling along the reefs. The ocean looked calm and inviting. We decided to go for a swim. I swam along the reef where the water was crystal clear. I could see little fish of all colors; it was fascinating. Fernando started yelling, "Hello, New York!" pointing at the horizon, which I gathered was the right direction. I yelled, "Hello, Les, Aunt Anna." I waved my arms and continued swimming in the same direction.

Fernando and I were separated by a large wave, which carried me farther out. I was mesmerized by all the strange-looking fish I could see in such clear water. I didn't realize how much time had passed. Fernando was quite a distance away. I began to swim toward him in the direction of the shoreline. The waves were hitting me from behind. I tried long strokes laterally. It did no good. I realized I was in trouble and waved my arms each time I surfaced; I yelled his name. He couldn't hear me. I had drifted too far away. I kept swimming, but the waves hit me from behind and dragged me underwater. I was tiring from swimming back up to the surface and was swallowing sea water. I was desperately alone, knocked under water over and over.

Caught in an undertow, I was thrown against the outer reefs. With my energy gone, I was hurled onto the coral and barnacles attached to the reef. I lashed back and forth, struggling after each wave to raise my head above water. A rescue swimmer with a white life-preserver attached to a long rope reached me. The rope was held tight by a human chain of people standing alongside the reef out to the depth of the ocean. The rescue swimmer relied on the support of the people for his own safety as well as the one being rescued, which in this case was me.

For the first time in my life, I was carried out of the water almost lifeless. My bathing suit was halfway torn off. I was embarrassed but could not help myself. They covered me with a sheet once on shore and administered oxygen in a white first aid tent with a large red cross on top. My wounds were cleansed and bandaged. It took hours in the tent to get my breathing back to normal. I had swallowed a huge amount of sea water.

Fernando was cut more than me, but he would not leave my side. He was so upset and nervous, hovering over me.

"You saved my life, Fernando," I finally said. "I will never forget this day." A crowd of people were gathered all around the tent. Later I found out several swimmers had drowned in the same spot earlier that summer. Also, this area was well known for riptides. The local people were warned not to swim out as far as we had gone. If we had only known. I prided myself in being a strong swimmer—until today. Fernando and I were so grateful to the rescue squad. It was a slow scooter ride back to the city. When we arrived at the university, I bid Fernando a good night. I was exhausted and so was he.

Monday morning, August 31st, Fernando came for our last breakfast together. He helped me carry my luggage to load my scooter. His eyes were watery. I wanted to give him a kiss on the cheek but realized, given the state of mind he was in, it would make matters worse. I gave him a strong hug goodbye. He looked so pitiful. "I'll write to you in California," he offered.

"I'll look forward to hearing from you. Thanks for a wonderful visit in Portugal. Take care of yourself, Fernando." My suitcases were fastened in place. I got on my scooter, pulled it from its stand, and took off not looking back.

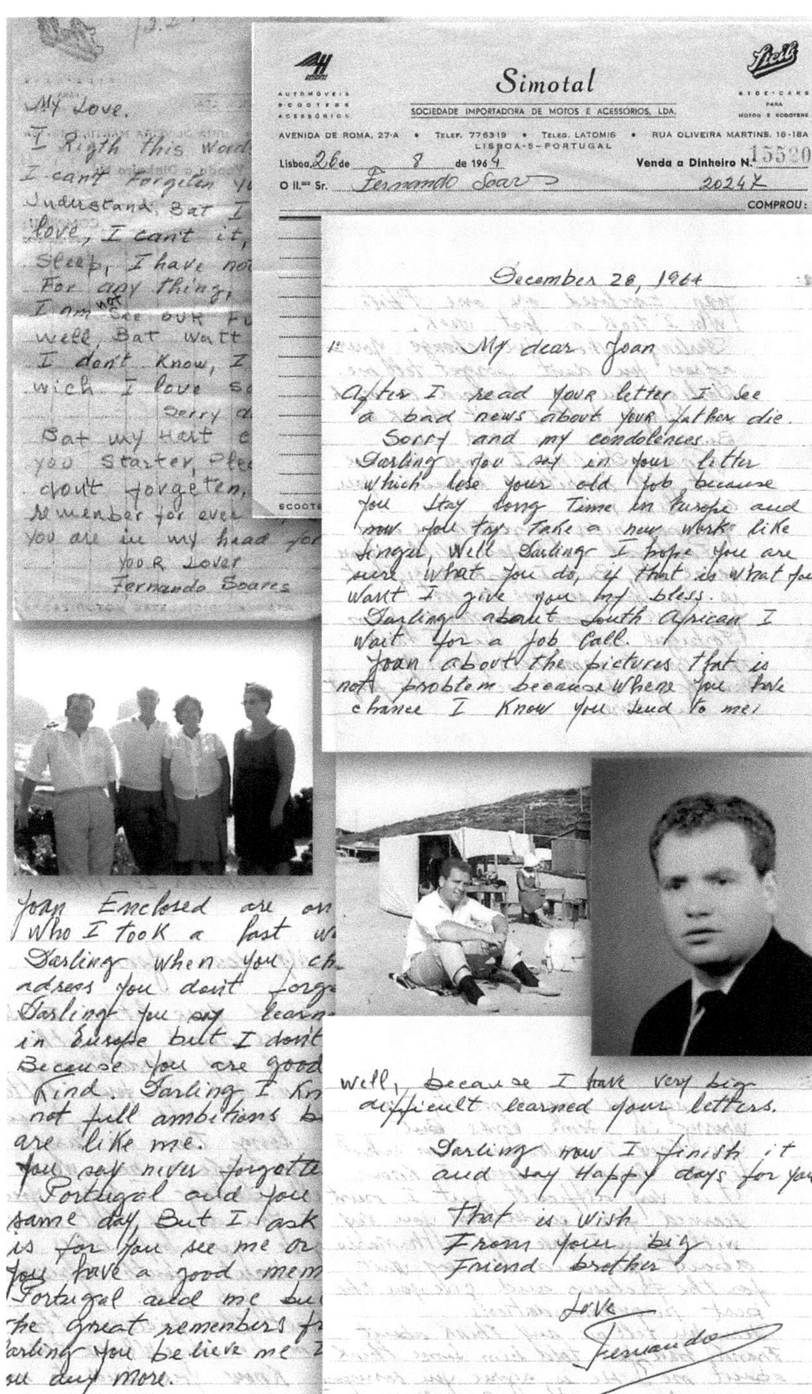
My Love.
I Rigth this Word...
I can't forgeten yo...
Understand, Bat I...
love, I cant it,...
Sleep, I have no...
For any thing,...
I am not see our f...
well, Bat watt...
I don't Know, I...
wich I love s...
Sorry d...
Bat my Hert c...
you starter, Ple...
don't forgeten,...
remember for ever...
you are in my head for...
Your Lover
Fernando Soares

Simotal
AUTOMÓVEIS SCOOTERS ACESSÓRIOS
SOCIEDADE IMPORTADORA DE MOTOS E ACESSÓRIOS, LDA.
SIDE-CARS PARA MOTOS E SCOOTERS
AVENIDA DE ROMA, 27-A • TELEF. 776319 • TELEG. LATOMIS • RUA OLIVEIRA MARTINS, 18-18A
LISBOA-5-PORTUGAL
Lisboa, 26 de 8 de 1964 Venda a Dinheiro N.º 15520
O Il.mo Sr. Fernando Soares 2024 K
COMPROU:

December 28, 1964

My dear Joan
After I read your letter I see a bad news about your father die.
Sorry and my condolences.
Darling you say in your letter which lose your old job because you stay long time in Europe and now you tays take a new work like singel, Well Darling I hope you are sure what you do, if that is what you want I give you my bless.
Darling about South African I wait for a job call.
Joan about the pictures that is not problem because where you have chance I Know you send to me.

Joan Enclosed are on...
Who I took a last w...
Darling when you ch...
adress you don't forg...
Darling you say learn...
in Europe but I don't...
Because you are good...
Kind. Darling I Kn...
not full ambitions b...
are like me.
You say never forgotte...
Portugal and you...
same day, But I ask...
is for you see me or...
you have a good mem...
Portugal and me bu...
the great remembers f...
Darling you believe me I...
...u day more.

well, because I have very big difficult learned your letters.
Darling now I finish it and say Happy days for you
That is wish
From your big
Friend brother
Love
Fernando

Simotal

AVENIDA DE ROMA, 27-A

TELEFONE 776319

LISBOA

Data ___ / ___ / 19___

Matricula

Marca

Kilóm.—Ent.

Kilóm.—Said.

Entregar ___ / ___ às ___ h.

NOME

MORADA

TELEF.

ARMAZÉM

Ordem de Reparação N.º 20247

Escritório

Linha	
1	LAVAGEM
2	LUBRIFICAÇÃ
3	PARAFINAÇÃO
4	MOTOR
5	CAIXA
6	TROCAR ROD
7	LAVAGEM DO
8	BATERIA
9	FOCAR FARÓIS
10	VÁLVULAS verificar e afinar

BILHETE DE ENTRADA 2$50 ESC.

PALÁCIO NACIONAL DE MAFRA

O edifício (Palácio, Basílica e Convento) foi mandado construir por D. João V, em cumprimento, segundo a tradição, de um voto para ter descendentes.
O projecto foi de J. F. Ludovice e nas obras (1717-35) chegaram a trabalhar 50.000 operários.
Tem valiosas esculturas, dois carrilhões, os maiores do Mundo, Museu de Arte Sacra, com riquíssimos paramentos e Biblioteca cuja sala (84 m) é das mais belas do País.

TELEFONE 77 52 17

PENSÃO UNIVERSITÁRIA

José Ribeiro

Av. 5 de Outubro, 289-3.º — LISBOA

Lisboa, 31 de 8 de 1964

O Ex.mo Sr.

DEVE

Diárias		
Dormidas 8	240	00
Alojamento		
Pequeno almoço 8	60	00
~~Almoço~~ uvas	4	00
Jantar		
Vinhos		
Cafés		
Roupa lavada	10	00
Banhos 2	12	00
Extraordinários		
	326	00
Taxa de Serviço 10%	32	60
	358	60

Chapter Ten: Central Spain

Along the four hundred kilometers to Trujillo, Spain, I thought a lot about Fernando, Cecilia, and my time spent in Portugal. The weather, as I drove along, felt like California—sunny and clear. I found a nice hotel, had dinner, and enjoyed some wine. As usual, I was feeling relaxed and tired, but I was looking forward to visiting Madrid the next day. My brother had been stationed there, and he loved it.

On my way to Madrid, a young man flagged me down by waving his arms in the middle of the road. I thought one of my suitcases had shifted and might be falling from the luggage rack. I stopped with my feet on the ground balancing my scooter with the engine running. I looked back and everything seemed in order. I didn't understand a word of his Spanish. He pointed to a river that was flowing beneath an underpass. I believe he wanted me to go swimming.

"*No comprendo,*" I said shaking my head.

By this time I was pretty sure that meant, "I don't understand." I gunned my engine on the handlebar and drove around him and his Fiat.

About twenty kilometers farther down the road, I saw him again in the middle of the road, waving his arms. I pulled to a stop. He rattled off more Spanish I didn't get. I started to drive around him. He had a big smile on his face as I pulled around his car about to take off. He held up a rubber prophylactic, nodding his head up and down, saying, "Si, si."

I was so provoked at his nerve, I gunned the engine until I was burning rubber on the road around him. I thought, *If only I would have had enough command of Spanish, I could have told him exactly what I thought!* I drove faster along the road and lost him before I got to the center of Madrid.

I was so excited to be in downtown Madrid! The streets were exceptionally clean, and I noted some department stores looking inviting. I pulled up along the curb to get leverage with my foot, enabling me to raise the scooter onto its stand. I got off the seat, leaned over to unhook my purse from beneath the steering column, and I heard, "Miss, you can't wear shorts here in downtown, or you will be arrested," stated a man in English, walking on the sidewalk.

"What? You mean I can't shop here?" I asked.

"No, there is an ordinance which doesn't permit women in shorts. And men must wear a tie when downtown," he added.

One of the few times I wore beige shorts due to the warm California-like weather, and it's not permitted. I was surprised, but I got back on my scooter, pushed it off its stand, and drove around the block a few times, looking for some place to change clothes. I couldn't find any place where I could safely park my scooter and run in to change. I was disappointed, because I really wanted to spend time in and around the city. My brother had talked about how fond he was of Madrid. I went a little farther out, canvasing the area for a hotel or gas station. I was outside the city limits before I knew it.

Disgusted, I drove another 113 kilometers. When I reached Granada, I stopped for the night. The city streets were very narrow; some streets had steps leading uphill. Most of the buildings aligning the narrow streets were adobe-colored, three-stories tall, with balconies above where people lived.

In Old Town, streets were so narrow you could put your arms out and touch the buildings on both sides at the same time. I walked a few blocks from the hotel to settle my dinner. A middle-aged man approached me speaking Spanish. I didn't understand his words and did not like his abrupt mannerisms or attitude. I began to walk more briskly to get ahead of him and entered my hotel.

That evening, when I got in bed I was on edge. I had the feeling that the man had followed me. I rolled back and forth for several hours, unable to sleep.

Suddenly, there was pounding on my door! I saw the door-knob move. I got scared and screamed, "Go away or I'll call the *policia*." Silence reigned for about an hour. I thought it had probably been that strange man I saw when I was outside. The room had no phone or inside latch on the door. The pounding began again. I could see the door jarring from force from outside. It was frightening. I got up and pushed the dresser against the door. I checked the window and it was fastened tight. I looked out and saw it wasn't too far of a jump below, in case I had to escape. I positioned my pillows and sat up in bed waiting for what was to come next. I was frantic with worry and knew I was on my own.

It was three o'clock in the morning when the banging began again. I yelled, "Get out of here or I'll call the police!" More loud pounding continued, and then it stopped. I lay there in a panic until daybreak. The first thing I did was get out my Spanish dictionary and start putting words together to report the incidents to the management. I was furious! Why didn't anyone hear my screaming or the banging on my door throughout the night? Prepared to check out early, I took my Spanish notes and approached the front desk.

"No me escuchaste gritar anoche?" (Didn't you hear me scream last night?) I rattled off. The people in the lobby stared at me as I continued raising my voice.

"Un hombre intentó derribar mi puerta tres veces diferentes. Qué tipo de ritmo es este?" (These were the words I put together attempting to say, "A man tried to break into my room three times. What kind of place is this?")

"No se de que estas hablando," (He looked embarrassed, but I wasn't sure what he was saying in Spanish.) He acted like he was stupid. I believe he knew what happened and didn't give a damn. I was so upset I threw down my key and said, "Give me

my bill." I glanced at the amount and threw down my pasetas (dollars). I rushed through the line of guests with two of my bags and stormed out the door. I loaded the two big suitcases and went back to get my cosmetic case.

Once fully loaded, I turned the key, gunned my engine—releasing the handlebar clutch too fast—and spun some gravel on my way out. I didn't mean to spin out of there, but I had just been through a nightmare. I had not been scared traveling alone until now. During this trip, traveling in the open air, I had felt so free and welcome everywhere. Now I would have to be more careful and make sure there was an inside bolt on all hotel doors. Also, I needed to be more discreet and not tell anyone I was traveling alone—not that I advertised the fact before, but it was obvious to anyone noticing my arrival by motor scooter.

I stopped for breakfast and could not get the danger of last evening out of my mind. I continued onward until eight o'clock that evening, when it was getting dark and chilly. I stopped for the night, freshened up, changed into a skirt, blouse, and flat shoes before going to the restaurant. I sat at a middle table among other guests trying not to bring any attention to my being alone. I secured the safety chain inside my door, but still felt insecure. It took a few hours for me to relax and fall asleep.

On Friday, September 4th, I had breakfast, loaded up the scooter, and off I went into the unknown. I arrived in Girona, Spain. I came across a modern, small hotel with a shower in my suite—a feature which was always an added pleasure. I placed my suitcases in my room without unpacking. I got back on my scooter. It was always fun to drive around without worrying about my suitcases shifting.

I looked for a garage to get a needed oil change. I found a garage with several motor scooters outside, motorcycles parked inside and at the curbside. Rober the mechanic spoke English, which was a plus. He was handsome, tall, well-built, with charcoal black wavy hair and dark brown eyes. I waited around until two that afternoon when it started to rain. My scooter was not finished. Rober agreed to house my scooter for the night and finish it in the morning.

"I'm sorry, I had too many cycles ahead of you. Since you have no transportation, I would be pleased to take you to dinner," he said, looking up from the garage floor. I had a feeling he was up to something, the way he kept looking at me as he reached for one tool or another. It seemed to me he was working awfully slow.

"Well, I suppose." I hesitated because of situations I had encountered before. He seemed like a gentleman. I thought to myself, *Why not, as long as it was within walking distance.* I pointed up the narrow road and gave him the name of my hotel.

"How's about my meeting you at six o'clock?" he offered with a smile.

"Fine. Are you sure my scooter is safe here until tomorrow?"

"Yes, you need not worry. I'll lock it inside the shop for the night."

"All right, then. I will be expecting you around six." I turned and looked back at my scooter, already having separation anxiety leaving it behind. If I lost it, I would have no means of getting back to Germany.

I stepped outside from the small lobby of the hotel around six that evening. The pavement was wet, and it felt like more rain was coming. An old antique limo drove up to the curb. I was surprised to see it was Rober. He got out of the old car and walked over to me. He said, "Come and see my pride and joy."

It was an old Willy's Limousine. He opened the passenger's door and I looked inside. It reminded me of my father's old Henry Kaiser car made in the 30's. The upholstering was dark gray, and the seats were high. It was mysterious looking.

"I want to take you to a nice restaurant on the lake. It isn't far from here."

"I thought we were going within walking distance," I said. Once again, I found myself in a difficult situation. I didn't want to embarrass him or have him think I didn't trust him.

"Don't worry, it isn't that far of a drive. You will really enjoy the food and the view of the lake. I do expect more rain," he explained. I had to make a quick decision without showing any fear outwardly. I got in reluctantly and was on my guard. He closed the heavy door behind me. It was just as he said—only a few blocks to the lake. It was fun getting into a car after traveling so many miles by scooter in the open air. The car was old and a kick to ride in.

The food was delicious, and I ate way too much. He asked me all about my life in California and said he hoped one day he would have the money to visit. It was a delightful evening and experience. He was a perfect gentleman, but, as I expected, he snuck a quick kiss when I turned my head toward him on the way back to my hotel. I didn't resist, for he was romantic and handsome. Had I not been promised to Paco, I might have encouraged more kisses, for I missed having some warm affection. The excitement of traveling kept my loneliness for Paco at bay.

"I must call it an evening, for I have a long day ahead tomorrow. Thank you for dinner and good company," I told him. He escorted me from the car to the lobby.

"I'll be down early, right after breakfast, to pick up my Heinkel," I said.

"It will be ready by nine o'clock. Thanks for a great time," he added. I could tell he had hoped for some romance, but it wasn't going to happen. I went to my suite and took advantage of a nice warm shower before bed. It wasn't often I had a private bath in my suite.

The next morning, I had breakfast and hurried to pick up my scooter from Rober. I was told he was called out on a job before I arrived. I had wanted to say goodbye, but I couldn't wait for his return. I paid my bill, drove back to the hotel, and loaded my baggage.

Chapter Eleven: Southern France to Germany

It was extremely dark, dreary weather all the way to the French border. I was directed by a Border Control agent to get off my scooter. I tried to explain by motioning that I needed to pull over near a curb to give me leverage to get it on its stand. If I got off my scooter it would fall to the ground, suitcases and all. He didn't understand my motioning about the curb. He was demanding with his French words. When I didn't comply, he placed his hand at his revolver. I had to demonstrate by getting halfway off how it would fall to the ground without my leg support. He finally realized I needed to pull over to the curb and stepped aside.

Once the scooter was on its stand, the agent asked for my passport, then directed me to open all my bags. It began to sprinkle rain. He rummaged through my clothes and found a tube of lip ice; he tore it apart. (I guess he thought it was a drug.) After messing up my clothes he motioned for me to go on.

I was furious! He was getting everything wet, but he had to show his superiority. I didn't like his attitude, and he knew it. I closed my suitcases, loaded them back on my scooter, and took off with a jolt to let him know I was more than provoked.

I drove farther into France and stopped to get gas and food. My Spanish pesetas and traveler's checks were refused. After four stops, I was disgusted with the French for refusing to accept my money. I decided to outsmart them. I filled my tank, and then I said, "Sorry, no Francs." The Frenchman was rattling off in French and I thought he was going to have me arrested.

Already, I was making a comparison between the French, Spanish and Portuguese. The Spanish and Portuguese people were warm and friendly, and the French uncooperative and arrogant. I couldn't wait to get out of the area. I drove another four hundred kilometers.

At six o'clock that evening, it started to pour down rain. I pulled my scooter under a straw roof by a hotel. When I unpacked my bags, I discovered all my clothes were soaked inside. I had to hang everything around the room to dry. The blue lining of my large suitcase faded onto my beige, soft leather purse. It was ruined.

Sunday, September 6th, the dark dreary weather continued. I drove two-hundred-fifty kilometers, which took another four hours in the rain. I was soaked, cold and miserable. I was just outside of Lyon, France, and didn't want to go farther. The hotel I found was expensive and upscale. I would have to make a complete change from a cold, wet, weary traveler to a professional-looking businesswoman in a suit and heels.

Suddenly someone was knocking on my door. I opened the door partway, and a young Frenchman pushed the door completely open, holding his razor in front of his face. He brushed past me, speaking French, then he stopped at my bathroom sink. I didn't understand a word he'd said. He turned, walked briskly back toward me, pinched up my cheek, slipped his other arm around my waist and attempted to French-kiss me. I pushed him back toward the open door. He looked surprised as I quickly attempted to force him out the door. He put his foot to block the door, leaning back, trying to kiss me again. I kicked the door against his foot, and he backed up. I slammed the door shut and fastened the chain. What a crazy man!

I took a deep breath and began to lay out my outfit for the evening. I was taking a spit bath at the sink, when someone rapped several times again, saying, "Mademoiselle, mademoiselle?"

I yelled, "Go away!" I continued with my bath when something made me look upward. That same man was looking in at me through the transom window above the door! I grabbed a towel to cover up, but it was too late; he'd already seen me in the nude. I yelled, "Get out of here!" I heard him laughing as he got down from the window. If only I could have somehow reported his behavior. If I spot him when I go out to dinner, I will advise the management.

On Monday, September 7th, I headed out in the rain again toward Germany. I had to stop under a cover for an hour due to heavy rain. I arrived at the German border wet and weary. At a speed of 80 km/h, the air felt like thirty-degree weather. I was anxious to get to Wiesbaden but couldn't risk getting a cold or pneumonia. I stopped early for the night at a hostel type of hotel. I ordered sauerkraut and pork, which hit the spot. I heard two young German men speaking English, and my ears perked up. They sent over an after-dinner drink and joined my table. It was fun speaking English and mostly listening to their boasting about their lives. I didn't reveal any information about my mode of travel due to my previous experiences.

Finally, I came to the autobahn; it was a welcomed sight. Several U.S. Army truck convoys passed by me. I smiled to myself, realizing I was getting closer to Wiesbaden.

The rain continued to pour down. It was so heavy it was stinging my face until I could barely see ahead. I parked in an underpass for almost two hours waiting for the rain to slack up. Trucks splashed me as they passed by. I thought I would never get out of there. Finally, the rain slowed down, and I drove farther to a *Restplatz* to warm up and get a snack.

Eventually the rain stopped, and the sky got brighter. I arrived at Jan's in Wiesbaden at three o'clock that afternoon. I parked my scooter in the grassy medium in front of Jan and Fran's flat. I removed the largest suitcase and carried it up five flights of stairs. Fran helped me with the rest of my luggage. They opened champagne, and we celebrated being together again. I shared some of my adventures thus far. I was relaxed being back among my American friends.

On Wednesday, September 9th, I took the train into Frankfurt to Bache & Company regarding cashing in AT&T stock certificates. I was told the cash would be available in five days. I walked quite a distance to find the shop where I had bought my scooter. I asked one of the shop owners if he could sell my Heinkel. Luckily, he was the one who spoke English well. He seemed happy to see me. I told him the scooter had carried me all over Europe and was very reliable. He smiled and responded, "Bring it in and we will sell it. We won't charge you any commission since you purchased it here."

"Thanks, that's kind of you," I replied. "I'll drive it over tomorrow and leave it."

I walked back to the bus stop to return to Wiesbaden. Jan was home and drove me in her boyfriend's car to the air base. I ordered my first cheeseburger since I had left the U.S. and had a hot fudge sundae with whipped cream. It was too much food, but I couldn't resist it.

That evening we went to visit Grandma. I was getting to know her better. She was only fifty-five, with medium-brown hair, about five foot five, and around 165 pounds. I found out the reason everyone called her "Grandma" was due to her carefree attitude. She loved to hang around the servicemen, prost beer, and party at the German restaurants. She was full of life, singing along with the accordion players in broken German. She had left her husband, an artist, in California because he didn't work and kept painting oils on every piece of canvas he could find. According to Grandma, he lived on cold cereals; he never ate regular meals.

"I got sick of his behavior and left him. I wanted to travel Europe, and here I am," she remarked. Her flat was on the third floor and she had a rope tied to her windowsill with clothes pins attached. She had no telephone and would write a message and attach it via a clothes pin on a rope on a pulley wheel. When she pulled the rope the clothes pin hit the lower window of her neighbor across the courtyard on the first floor. Val, her neighbor, would open the window and shout, "I'll be right up." At times she would answer the note and send it back up via the rope. Grandma drove around in a VW Pop Top Camper, which she used for camping and traveling around Germany

Friday morning, September 11th, I drove my scooter to Frankfurt to the dealer. This was my last trip, and I hated to leave it. The cost to ship it to the states was out of the question. My hope was they could sell it quickly, for my funds were low. Riding the train, I pictured in my mind how I had learned to drive it through the Alps, dumping it and having to learn the hard way. Oh, how I missed my scooter already! My neck was stiff and I was beginning to have cold symptoms. No wonder—after driving through a cold rain for a few days.

When I got back to the flat, Jan and Bob had returned from their honeymoon. Bob would be shipped to Turkey, and Jan would return to California. Jan looked like she had lost weight. Their return made a total of four of us sharing the flat. If Frau Goring found out we were all sleeping there, we would be in trouble.

Jan would leave for the states in October. Fran had been coaxing me to extend my trip and drive her 1956 Opal to pick up her mother and aunt in Holland. Fran had been practicing driving the narrow streets around Wiesbaden. Her coordination between the steering wheel and brake was questionable. She drove us up over curbs and was slow to steer out of the way of oncoming traffic. We didn't have enough time between the present and her mother's visit for her to get the needed experience.

The plan was to drive her loved ones to visit their homeland in Norway. Fran agreed to pay all the travel expenses. I would be responsible for my own meals.

"I promised to take Mom and my Aunt May to Norway after they retired. I can't disappoint them," Fran explained. Apparently, they had been planning on Fran doing this for years. Fran bought the old Opal and tried to learn to drive, but time had run out. Feeling sorry for her, I thought to myself, *Spending another six weeks or so wouldn't be so bad. After all, I would be able to visit countries I have not yet seen.*

I eventually said, "Okay, Fran, I'll help you out. I realize how important this trip is for you, your mother, and aunt."

"Joan, I promise, you won't be sorry, and we will have a good time," Fran responded.

I followed with, "Since I'm the driver we need to have the car checked over. We will be covering a lot of miles. I recommend taking it to the Opal dealer for servicing. Also, the tires need to be checked."

"No problem; I'll make an appointment. The Opal dealer is close by," Fran went on.

Finally, I got a chance to be alone and do a sink bath. There had been so much traffic in and out of there, I was lucky to be able to grab the sink long enough to brush my teeth.

Jan and I drove to the base to do our laundry. We stopped by the snack bar and I had an old-fashioned hamburger. I followed with an ice cream cone. It was great to have some American food for a change. My cold was still hanging on. I got a letter from Aunt Anna. It was good news; my cousin Andy moved out of the tenant house I used to rent. What a relief to find out my old, little house was available to go back to when I returned to California. There was no mail from Paco.

Fran and Bruce, her boyfriend, took me sightseeing in Wiesbaden. The Russian church overlooking the city with its bright gold domes, followed by the famous Coor House were among our first visits. They drove me around the large park near there. The weather felt much like October in Pennsylvania.

Fred was waiting at the flat when we returned. He took me to the base theatre to see *Good Neighbor Sam* with Jack Lemon. Afterward we went to the snack bar for a malt. I savored it; it had been months since I'd had one.

Tomorrow I would have to purchase car insurance for the trip. I went to turn in my Heinkel license plate and apply for car insurance for Fran's old car. I found out a road tax of fifty-seven German marks would be charged. I wasn't sure about paying it. I walked over to where Jan worked and was told the tax had to be paid.

Right before lunch, an Egyptian by the name of Sheata came to the flat. He invited me to lunch. Afterwards he kissed me on both cheeks. Now I can say I've been kissed by an Egyptian—what a life! He spoke with strange, broken English and called me Lady Joan. He asked me out on a date, and I made excuses. It seemed there was always someone trying to wine and dine me; they never got it when I told them I was promised to Paco.

To finish the paperwork for the Opal, I drove back to Biebrick. I discovered the engine number didn't agree with the title papers. The gentleman spoke English well and said Fran had paid too much for the car.

I stopped for gas on my way back to Wiesbaden. The man who put the gas in the car introduced himself as Addie. He was good looking, with dark brown hair, about six foot, a great masculine frame, and a very sincere smile. He said, "I'll fix the car and ensure it is in good shape for you for no money. I would like it if you give me Old Spice from the Base Exchange." I agreed. He worked on the car for over an hour.

"I'll bring the after-shave lotion tomorrow," I explained. Then I thought, *I wish it were this easy in America to get something done on your car.* Fran and Bruce got a charge out of my bargaining with Addie. They took me over to Grandma's for pizza and wine. Fran had another bird for Grandma; it would be a companion for her other Finch.

On Thursday, September 17th, I went to the post office looking for a check from the stock shares I had sold. I had received a statement the shares were sold, and a check would follow later. I ran back to the flat trying to dodge a downpour. I didn't make it in time, and I got soaked.

Jan and I tried baking a cake in little glass pie dishes. I went back out to the store looking for brown sugar; I couldn't find any. I had to go to several places before I found ice cream. The pastries in the shops were well displayed and looked delicious. I wished we had pastry shops like that in America. The crazy cakes we baked didn't taste too bad. Bruce and Fred came by and I told them that the Opal engine number was not in agreement with the paperwork. They went down to the street to check the numbers and found the two numbers in fact did not coincide.

The following day, Jan and I went to Biebrich to get the license for the Opal. It was easier than we thought. They changed our paperwork to agree with the engine number. Charlie had wrecked Jan's 1950 Mercedes, and it looked like Jan's insurance would not cover it—all due to Charlie being under twenty-one years old. Charlie was one of our young airmen protecting our country and stationed in Germany. From what I heard, our servicemen and women did not like the Germans. They would count the days until their tour was over and they could return to the states.

I met up with Val and Grandma, and we went to the Rocco NCO club. I won fourteen quarters in the slot machine. Val said, "I watch the machines being played. When I see a machine has not paid off for a while, I play it and many times win."

We met four men from Pennsylvania who sent drinks over to us and followed us to the Jockey Club. We all were feeling no pain, and the M.C. of the floor show got a big kick out of my laugh. It was a fun time.

On Monday, September 21st, I went back to the post office. I had letters from home, Paco's family, and Serge, but none from Paco. He was probably upset because I didn't stay with his mother. Later, I went to see Addie about the Opal repairs. He asked me to join him for dinner.

"Leave the car here and I'll check it over tomorrow," Addie advised. I agreed and gave him the Old Spice he'd wanted from the Base Exchange; he was pleased. Later we met, and he took me to a nice restaurant where it was a candlelit romantic atmosphere. We both had too much wine. He confessed, "I think I'm in love with you and want to buy you a ring. Then you will not forget me."

"Addie, I've told you; I'm promised to a man back in America. You have had too much to drink."

"No, I haven't," he protested, "and I know what I want in a woman. Please take me seriously."

"I'm sorry," I replied. "I find you attractive and a nice gentleman. But this can only be your imagination. It's due to me being from America and different than most German women you know. You will find that perfect woman you're looking for, but it isn't me." I thought, *I always end up having these men think they are in love with me. Can't I just be friends with a man? I certainly don't try to attract attention.*

He was sad when we left the restaurant. When we arrived at Jan's apartment house he said, "If you don't want to stay in Germany, I could come to the U.S."

Our eyes met as he opened the car door for me. I realized at that point I was vulnerable. I had been away from Paco for months. Addie was very handsome and romantic. I had to be on my guard.

"By the way, Joan, don't forget to buy me some size-five Jockey underwear and ice cream from the exchange," he remarked with a smile.

I returned the smile and quickly stepped away from his car. "I won't forget," I replied. As I trudged up the five flights of stairs to Jan's flat, I realized I would have to keep my distance in the future, for I felt attracted to him. I was tipsy and sat outside the door waiting for Jan or Fran to come home since I had no key.

The following morning, I picked up the old Opal, and Fran and I went to meet Fred. On our way to the base, the car broke down. I removed the air filter and had Fran pump on the accelerator. I pushed it and we coasted downhill, but it wouldn't start. We walked the rest of the way to the base. It was a cool day that reminded me of late October in Pennsylvania. We caught a cab from the base to the Opal Haas to see Addie. He had one of his men drive us back to the car. The mechanic fixed it in about ten minutes; the carburetor filter was clogged. I drove the Opal back to the garage. Addie replaced the filter and I went to the Post to see if my check had arrived. Thank heavens, it was there, but no other mail. I had thirty-eight dollars between me and poverty. I took the train to Frankfurt and checked on my scooter at the dealer. They told me a man was interested but it had not sold yet.

On Saturday, September 26th, I walked the couple of blocks from the flat to the garage. It was shortly after eight o'clock when

I saw Addie. He ran out to meet me and explained, "I greased the car, changed the spark plugs, and checked it all over for you. Now, will you go out with me this evening?"

I handed him a package of Jockey undershorts. Our eyes met. I paused before answering, "No, I really can't this evening. As I said before, I like you as a friend and appreciate all you are doing to get Fran's car ready for our trip, but that's it."

"Joan, please!" he persisted. "You are hurting my feelings. Why can't we have a nice meal together? I just want to get to know you better."

"Addie, we have been over this before. I've got to go. Thanks for checking over the car." I quickly turned and opened the car door without looking back. In my rear view mirror I saw him look so disappointed but I just cannot promote this relationship.

That evening, I heard a rap at Jan's apartment door. I opened the door to find Addie standing there. I made him a cup of coffee. Fran came home, and she and Addie got into an argument about Hitler.

"I had relatives in Holland that suffered during the war," Fran told him. "And Switzerland was a neutral country, but Hitler didn't care that it provided neutrality. He took everyone's possessions, raided the museums for the artwork, and dragged the Jewish people to camps. At Dachau and many other concentration camps, the Nazis had the Jews dig ditches; then the Nazis machine-gunned them down. The Jews fell into the graves they had just finished digging."

"I was a young boy, and we didn't know about the Concentration Camps. When I saw my relatives in uniform who fought for Germany, I felt proud," Addie explained.

Fran was getting very irritated. I broke up the argument: "Come, Addie, I've got to go down and move the Opal to a better spot for the night. I don't want to get a traffic ticket." I ushered him out the door and practically ran down the five flights with him trying to catch up.

I hugged him goodnight and sent him on his way. He didn't resist when I said, "It's okay, Addie. We all realize what a horrible war it was for everyone. In a short while, several airmen will arrive from the base here. It would not go well for you."

I moved the car to a regular parking spot and returned to the flat. Fred, Tom, Jan, Bob, Bruce, and a couple of Australians showed up for a party. Nine of us were in the flat. We started drinking and laughing. This was Jan's last evening before returning to the States. Frau Goring would have had a fit if she had seen all of us in that apartment. We gave everyone strict instructions as they left to be quiet going down the stairs past her flat and not disturb her.

On Wednesday, September 30th, Jan's husband, Bob, Tom, and I drove Jan to the airport. What a strange feeling, standing at the German airport watching my friend, Jan, leave for Los Angeles. I had a flashback of the years when I had gone to an airport, train, or bus terminal; I had always wished I were going somewhere. For once, I was not envious to go somewhere for I was still somewhere. I had a feeling of contentment for the first time.

I cooked lunch back at the flat for Bob and Tom. It was strange to have Jan gone. Bob would be transferred to Turkey. Fran, Fred, and I would leave for Holland tomorrow. We went out to the Oberbyran; about twenty of us, including Grandma, prosted drinks. Everyone was singing along with the accordion player; it was fun.

Every time they delivered a drink to our table, they placed a pencil slash on my cardboard coaster. Several people left without paying. Guess who ended up paying for all the slash marks on the coasters? Me!

It was two o'clock in the morning when I tried to sneak quietly up the five flights of stairs. I was paying special attention to the stair that squeaks, right by Frau Goring's flat, when Frau opened her door abruptly, yelling, "Who goes there?" I kept right on going. She looked up and saw me. *C'est la vie!* Thank heavens this would be my last night up to the fifth floor.

Jerry came in the morning and we helped Fran pack. She boxed some of her clothes to send back to the states. Frau Goring came up to check over the flat. She announced, "There have been too many people staying here. Look at my couch! It is sagging due to your guests staying here night after night. This flat was for two people, and you know it!"

"We have scrubbed the counters and floors for you. You should be grateful for that much," Fran blurted out. Frau grumbled and busied herself checking the bedroom. Fran and I had to hold back our laughter when she went into the bedroom. When she left the flat, we burst out loud laughing. We gathered up Fran's belongings. Several trips up and down the five flights of stairs took effort. On the last trip down we looked at one another and smiled. This was our last trip, and we wouldn't be returning.

We went to the bank to cash Fran's check and walked to Edith's for the night. She served an old-fashioned American meal. We slept in sleeping bags.

The next morning we delivered a suitcase of Fran's clothing to the post office to mail off to New York. Later, we packed up the Opal hoping to leave Wiesbaden by noon. We didn't pick up Fran's friend, Fred, until eight o'clock that night to start our journey to Holland.

Chapter Twelve: Belgium

On Friday, October 2nd, Fred drove three hundred kilometers until we reached the outskirts of Brussels. It was in the wee hours of the morning when we finally checked into a small hotel with a double and single bed. Fran and I shared the double bed and Fred took the single. The room had no heat, which was a warning of what was to come. After breakfast we went window shopping. The store windows were bright with fashion and prices too hefty for me. But the pastry shops were so enticing, we stopped for some. Fred's driving made me nervous, and I would have gladly taken the wheel.

Brussels proved to be an interesting, bustling city. We came across a large parade at the palace. We went sightseeing and came across a scale which revealed my weight was up ten pounds since I had left California. I knew I needed to cut back on all the food.

We drove through the countryside, which had not turned to fall on our way to Rotterdam. The apartment buildings along the street all had glass fronts from floor to ceiling. As we drove past, we could peer straight into the sitting rooms of the Dutch. The cafés' businesses were bright and cheery. It was as though everyone was inviting us in. I believe this was one of the brightest and cleanest of the countries I had visited thus far. We found a small hotel on the beach where young people were riding horseback along the coast. Walking along the beach reminded me of California beaches—except for the horses trotting by.

"Let's go to Madoradam," Fred suggested.

"That's a great idea; Joan hasn't been there," Fran said. Both Fred and Fran had already visited this park displaying the country of Holland in miniature. You walk along in a park like Disneyland, but everything was doll-like and at your feet. Little boats move along canals, windmills are moving in the countryside by farmhouses. It was very cleverly done. Fran took a picture of Fred and me bending down by one of the miniature scenes. We pushed on toward Amsterdam. Once again, the shops were bright and inviting with me wishing I had more money to spend. I stared at the beautiful topaz rings in the jewelry windows. Afterward, Fred drove Fran into the inner city so she could visit old friends she used to live with in Amsterdam.

The next day we drove through Amsterdam and found Hotel Hoksbergen, which was located adjacent to a canal. Our plan was to stay here for a few days. We went sightseeing, shopping, and taking in typical Dutch restaurants. Fred and Fran ordered raw roast beef sandwiches. I was hesitant, for the buns were soaked red from bloody meat. Fran told me, "You have got to try one of these sandwiches; they are delicious."

I paused while I watched a chef in the window make one after another. It wouldn't be the first time on this trip I tasted food I wasn't used too.

"Okay, give me one of those," I asked. I had to overlook the bloody bun as I bit into the sandwich. But Fran was right; it was delicious. Whether or not one should eat bloody raw beef was a question left unanswered. But it was so good I wouldn't hesitate to order one again in the future.

The day arrived for us to pick up Ruth, Fran's mother, and her Aunt May from Brooklyn, New York. Ruth was about five foot seven and thin; she had dark hair and a very stern look about her. She was dressed in dark slacks, a mink three-quarter length coat, and a mink hat. She was definitely prepared for colder weather.

Aunt May was short, rather plump, with a pleasant, rounded face. Strands of her white hair were sticking out beneath her mink hat. Both women looked as though they had just arrived from a winter season in upper Russia. They were very talkative and kept interrupting one another. I thought, *Boy, this will be quite a trip with everyone trying to get a word in edgewise.*

We took them shopping, and I purchased pajamas, a heavy, brown knit sweater, and a scarf. The five o'clock traffic was lined up at the signal lights of the wide streets. I couldn't believe all the bicycles, motor bikes, and scooters, side by side, waiting at the stop light.

"There are about ten million people here in Holland, and three million travel by bicycle," Fran explained. Trails ran along the main streets and highways specifically for bikes and motor scooters, which were impressive. I thought we should have bike trails like that in America.

The next morning I made a special trip to purchase wool socks to wear to bed to keep my feet warm. I picked up a pair of slacks for colder weather and a blouse. That evening we went to a restaurant where Danny Kaye and Esther Williams had eaten, called D'Vijff Vlieghe. It was established in 1627, and it was also known as the "Five Flies." They placed an American flag in the center of our table to represent our native country. My dinner was six dollars in American money, which was more than I can afford. I had to budget, while Fran and her relatives may not have had to.

We changed our itinerary to Norway and Copenhagen. It looked as though there were going to be differences of opinion because of our ages. I noticed that Fran started to stutter whenever her mother disagreed with her.

We stopped at the Lucky Star Club, which was a dive. We had dinner and cocktails and got back to the hotel at two o'clock in the morning.

Fran and I arose from our beds early. We looked out the window and saw that it was raining, so we went back to bed. When I got up later, I exercised a bit in the room thinking about all the weight gain. It was cold in our room, so I walked down to the hearth in the sitting room near the fire. I didn't go out until nine o'clock that night to get my favorite foods, croquettes, a salad, and a sandwich. The rest of the evening I sat on my bed with a towel wrapped around my neck to keep warm. Fred came by and stayed until eleven that night. I took two aspirins because I was cold one minute and hot the next, and I worried about getting another cold. The canals and rainy weather cause a penetrating kind of cold, and the lack of heat in our room was making it difficult to get warm.

On Thursday, October 8th, the sun was out but it was cold. I went to an antique shop and bought a few souvenirs for back home. I washed my hair and plucked my brows. Fran and Ruth had another argument; I could hear them shouting in the next room. Fran came over to our room afterward, stuttering and complaining about differences in the itinerary. Fran and I went out for dinner without them. We got soaked running back in the rain and were late to bed again.

Fred came to say goodbye; his leave from the Air Force base was over. He had the weekend to return to Wiesbaden, Germany. It was sad seeing him off to the train station. We had shared a lot of good times together over these past weeks.

Later we took Ruth and May to the Rijk's Museum. I stood and stared at many of Rembrandt's paintings. When I saw his "Night Watch," which was twenty feet tall and twenty feet wide, I was drawn into his canvas. I sat down on the bench in front of Rembrandt's life-like figures. Every detail was perfect. I spent several hours viewing the work of Rembrandt, Culp, and Monet. To realize I was traveling and still able to see such works of art was remarkable.

We left to catch a tram back to our hotel. It was pouring rain again. I got wet between the tram stop and a bite to eat. I took some movies of the bikes and scooters lined up across the wide streets; they were so amazing. I could only hope they turned out, in such bad weather. Back at the hotel I packed my bag to head for Hamburg, in North Germany, the next day.

On October 10th, Saturday, we didn't get started out until half past one that afternoon. Thank heavens we had plastic to protect the suitcases roped to the roof rack. I drove about three hundred kilometers. Then we found a nice Gasthaus for the night. My portion of the cost was $4.50 in American money, which covered my lodging and food. Feather quilts were on the beds to keep warm. The rooms, once again, were without heat, but the restaurant was warm with good food.

Chapter Thirteen: To Denmark

We enjoyed our last looks at the windmills leaving Holland. It was afternoon when we drove into Hamburg, Germany. I telephoned my friend, Will, whom I had met at work in Hollywood. Will's father gave me a number to call where Will was visiting a friend. Will was surprised to hear from me. He said, "Joan, I can't believe you really made it. Unfortunately, I won't be back in the city for a few days. Can I count on us getting together on your return trip from Norway?"

"Yes, of course, I will be in touch on our way back into Germany," I replied. It was good to hear his voice and talk about old times.

I stopped at a pastry shop for a hot chocolate and a delicious apricot Danish. Fran, her mother, and her aunt had coffee along with pastries. I drove one and a half hours to Odense, Denmark. We kept looking out the windows for a hotel to stop in for the night. We drove alongside two gentlemen and asked them for directions to a hotel. They appeared to be feeling no pain with a few drinks under their belts. We followed them down a few streets, then we lost them. We noticed Hotel Ansgar and stopped. It was already eleven o'clock. I lucked out; $2.50 was my portion of the bill. This included a continental breakfast, which was within my budget. Our destination the next day was Copenhagen.

Our first stop that day was Hans Christen Andersen's House. His original furniture, drawings, and pictures were on display. All the surrounding houses were small and quaint, appearing as though they were freshly painted.

The rain started again as we drove into the city of Copenhagen. The hotel we chose had an open smorgasbord with lots of choices. We walked down the street to the Ragol Hotel Bar. The men there made some remarks we didn't understand, but by their grimaces it wasn't that complimentary; too bad we weren't able to translate.

We left and drove to Maxims, where Jan used to work before she moved to Wiesbaden. We were curious after hearing from Jan about her time there. The private booths were upholstered a brilliant red velvet like settees in a French film. The walls were wall papered with colorful French scenes, and I noticed long, dark red, heavy silk drapes to the floor at the few windows. Girls dressed in short costumes and thigh-high, black, laced stockings were shifting from the bar to the booths. According to Fran, men paid for all the drinks as they visited with women, whether at the bar or at the tall, luxurious booths. Some couples would get up and disappear—I guess for prostitution. Other women made money by attracting men to buy them drinks, which, according to Fran, were watered down. But men were charged full price. Two men from Brooklyn, New York, sent us over drinks which cost thirty Kroner. We nodded to them a thanks, drank our drinks, and quickly left before they noticed.

I drove around the city for over one hour trying to find the Carlsberg Brewery. Once there, we enjoyed a tour of the building.

Afterward, we stopped at a nice restaurant. Four young men from the U.S. started talking with us. They suggested we go with them to the Britannia Pub. At the pub, men were throwing darts and smoking pipes. Later we went to the Vingarden, a jazz place. It reminded me of The Pitcher House in Redondo Beach, California, with bicycle fenders hanging from the ceiling, old license plates and memorabilia throughout. We drank beer, and everyone had a relaxing time. Copenhagen does have a lot going for itself.

The next morning, we went to see the The Little Mermaid statue at the water's edge. The picture of the famous mermaid was misleading. Postcards and travel brochures make the mermaid appear much larger. I crawled out onto the base of the statue so Fran could take a picture. I tried a balancing act trying to jump back to shore and almost fell in the water.

We later visited Frederick's Mormon Church and Palace on our way out of Denmark.

I drove more than three hundred fifty kilometers to reach Uddevalla, Sweden. Along the highway, the autumn leaves on the trees were bright colors of yellow and crimson. I drove the old Opal onto the ferry to cross the Nord Sea from Denmark to Sweden. I had to remind myself where I was; who would have thought I would one day be crossing the Nord Sea?

We stopped at a small village with a bubbling brook behind the hotel. They had steak and fries for dinner, along with a sundae for dessert.

Driving on the left side of the road is a real challenge. Every time I stopped, I had to remind myself to get on the left side of the road.

We passed barns and farmhouses with bright autumn leaves still on the trees. If I didn't realize this was Sweden, it could have been somewhere in the Pennsylvania woods.

On Thursday, October 15th, we headed for Norway. This was where Ruth and May had dreamed of visiting for years. This was where their ancestors were from. As we drove over a gorge I pulled over and took some movies with my Brownie.

It was great to be driving on the right side of the road again. The tall pine trees and mountains of Norway are vast and impressive. It was cooler and there was a feeling of fall. I drove about eighty-five km/h, and the car was humming along.

Oslo is a port city, and we had many things to see there. We stopped at a tourist center which referred us to a hotel with a huge room for four. Our individual cost was about a dollar and a quarter in Kronors. This was truly a bargain.

Ruth and May wanted to see the Viking ships. They were preserved, wooden ships that had sailed back in 900 A.D. Wooden sleighs from about the same period were displayed.

We visited a medieval castle from the 1300s on the waterfront. Afterwards, we toured through the Norwegian Folk Museum where old houses and barns were displayed from the twelfth century. The buildings had Lappish skis, sleds, costumes, furniture, and old utensils.

It was much colder up here, but the driving around Oslo was easy. I navigated around the port, and all the ships were in dry dock. We stopped at the Royal Palace, which was close to our hotel. Our dinner was equivalent to three American dollars, a great meal for the price. I overate again.

The shops weren't as bright and enticing as in Holland or Denmark. We walked around the city and drove out to the Hollenkamp Ski Jump where athletes practiced for the Olympics. I drove about fifty kilometers north to enjoy the beautiful mountains, then returned us to our hotel.

Ruth and May decided to leave the next day and return to Sweden. I guess all the mountains and beautiful countryside weren't enough excitement for them. Rather than having another argument, Fran went along with what they wanted. Fran's mother even made me upset with her "higher than thou" attitude. Ruth was domineering and critical of Fran. Lord knows what Ruth and May think of me, and it doesn't matter. I learned a few words in Norway, like *Tusatak* and *Mangatak,* meaning "thank you" and "many thanks."

Our last stop was to see the *Fram,* the ship which, during an expedition, discovered the North Pole. It was one o'clock that afternoon when we left Oslo. We stopped outside of Uddevalla at the same restaurant we had enjoyed on our way to Oslo. They had a buffet of about fifteen different kinds of fish, potatoes, cheeses, and eggs. I began to feel lightheaded after tasting so many kinds of fish. I had skipped lunch trying to lose some weight; maybe I shouldn't have.

On Monday, October 19th, we headed back to Copenhagen. On the way to Denmark, I drove onboard two different ferries, and then I continued for five hundred kilometers. Once again, I got lost in Odense. Our hotel stop was the New York Missions

Hotellet. We all agreed it was a goodbye to Sweden and a relief to get back to driving on the right. Our last ferry crossing was at nine-thirty that night. I continued for seventy kilometers in the fog of Denmark, which was surrounded by water; it's no wonder they have heavy fog.

It was eleven o'clock the following morning when Fran and I got the luggage loaded onto the car roof. We were heading for Hamburg again. We arrived at six-thirty that evening.

I freshened up and telephoned my friend Will. It had been so long since I'd seen Paco; it would be nice to spend an evening with male companionship with no worry of unwelcome advances. Ruth, May, and Fran went out to dinner, while I tried to reach Will. I waited for him to return my call. I was disappointed when no return call came. I skipped going out for dinner and went to bed. I would head the old Opal toward Berlin the next day.

The hotel notified me the next morning I had a telephone call. It was Will, advising me that he had telephoned several times last evening, but the hotel had informed him that I went out. I was upset about the mistake. Will said, "I'll come over and at least we can visit for a while."

"That's great; it'll be good to see someone from home," I replied.

Will stayed for almost two hours and visited with all of us. Everyone enjoyed talking with him about living in Hollywood and transitioning back home to Hamburg.

"I'll see you back in California," he promised. We said our goodbyes and I was sorry I didn't get a chance to have him show me around Hamburg the night before. Hamburg, being a large port city, turned out to be dreary and cold.

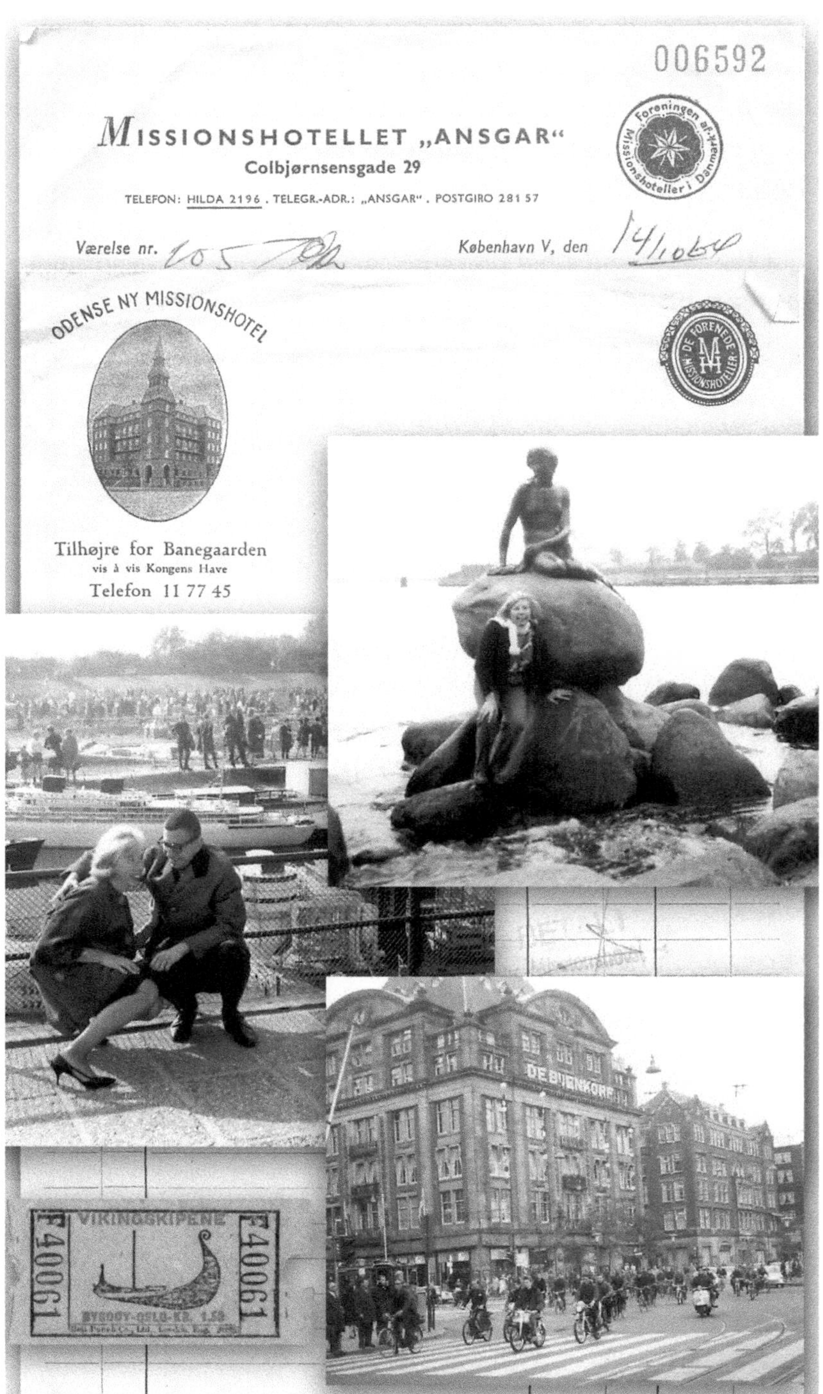
006592
MISSIONSHOTELLET „ANSGAR“
Colbjørnsensgade 29
TELEFON: HILDA 2196 . TELEGR.-ADR.: „ANSGAR“ . POSTGIRO 281 57
Værelse nr.
København V, den
Foreningen af Missionshoteller i Danmark
ODENSE NY MISSIONSHOTEL
Tilhøjre for Banegaarden
vis à vis Kongens Have
Telefon 11 77 45
DE FORENEDE MISSIONSHOTELLER
DE BIJENKORF
VIKINGSKIPENE
F40061
F40061

"EXCELLENT"

Hotel „West-End" about 100 KMS from amsterdam

Restaurant „St. Hubèrt"

Eig.: Fam. H. G. M. Mulder

Amsterd. weg 505 ARNHEM Tel. 08308-203 Giro 1726993

Kamer No. 37

HOTEL - CAFÉ-RESTAURANT

VAN WALSUM

Eig.: T. VAN DAM & ZOON

Mathenesserlaan 199, Rotterdam-3 - Telefoon 23 70 35 - Giro 24 83 90

Bank: Ned. Middenstandsbank, Bijkantoor Westersingel 19

...ember 1965

...ken en diversen

Bedrag

5,10

8,60

Hotel-Restaurant

„Van Walsum" № 223

Mathenesserlaan 199 - Rotterdam - Tel. 010 - 237035

Diverse Bitters			
Holl. Likeuren			
Bier			
Limonade			
Jus d'Orange			
Chocomel/Appelsap			
Port/Sherry/Vermouth	1		1 –
Franse Cognac/Whisky			
Buitenl. Likeuren			
Koffie/Thee			
Wijnen			
Keuken			
Lunch			
Diner			
Diversen			

Datum 10/11

Kamer no. 37

D...

JA...

RUM MAT CAFÉ

STICHTING TOT BIJSTAND VAN HET
NEDERL. STUDENTEN SANATORIUM
MINIATUURSTAD „MADURODAM"
077022
Volwassenen 1.25
(Sted. Bel. Inbegrepen)
Op verzoek aan bel.cont. tonen
Geen toegang zonder controlestrook
Madurodam
Den Haag

Chapter Fourteen: Berlin

We left for Berlin at one o'clock in the afternoon. When we arrived into Luneburg, Germany, we were told we had to have visas to drive into Berlin. I drove 150 kilometers out of our way to Helmstedt, Germany, to apply for visas. It took over an hour with the Russians to get the visas issued. We had to count out our currencies and list them on a form.

Ruth started complaining: "I'm not listing all my money for them!"

"Ruth, you can ignore their request, but I'm not," I said.

Fran warned her with, "You had better do as they say, because they can make trouble for us getting into East Berlin."

"I don't care, I'm not going to all that trouble," Ruth went on. May looked perplexed and wasn't sure what she was going to do. She usually followed what Ruth dictates.

"Hurry up, Joan. What's taking so long?" Ruth asked.

"I have a lot of different coins from so many countries, and I have to list them," I snapped back. I didn't care what she thought; I was following instructions and wanted no trouble from the Russians. Val, back in Wiesbaden, had told me stories about her encounters entering East Berlin. She had dealings with Russian guards at "Checkpoint Charlie" numerous times.

We got our visas and drove through the East Zone controlled by the Russians. I had to get out of the car at a checkpoint. They made me open the trunk, and I was scared they might lift the floorboard covering the spare tire where the stash of cartons of American cigarettes were hidden. My heart was pounding with fear of discovery. Also, I had many quarts of oil in the trunk. The Opal gobbled up a quart of oil about every five hundred kilometers.

I was ready to tell Ruth and May to keep their big mouths shut—although I wouldn't have put it exactly in those words if they started complaining while the Russians were checking our passports. I had to drive over mirrors on the road. The guards were carrying machine guns and appeared to be very sober men. I had an awful feeling of insecurity.

It was a two-hour drive to the western sector. The road was divided with two lanes on each side, deserted and very bumpy. I noticed only two gas stations along the entire scary road.

I was relieved when we reached the road in the western sector controlled by the Germans. They were friendly, and Fran spoke German to them, which helped break the ice.

The ol' opal had made it once again. I found Berlin to be an ultramodern city alongside old ruins still standing from the war. The shops were bright like Amsterdam. Everything was so upbeat it made me feel like Christmas was near. The West Germans were very friendly and bustling about. It was a vivid reminder to me about World War II when I saw the "Wall." The Russians claimed the wall was to protect the East Germans, when in fact it was to keep them penned up. The Germans from the West could visit East Berlin for the day but must leave before midnight.

Oh, to be rich! A person could really have a shopping spree here. My budget could barely afford a few souvenirs for relatives back home. Our hotel had a private bath—another welcome relief for a change. I went to the Deutsch Opera House, but they were sold out for Verdi's Troubadour. The next day we would take a bus tour of East Berlin that guaranteed a safe return.

What an experience, looking out the window as the bus drove through Checkpoint Charlie, where Russian soldiers stood guard with machine guns hanging from a leather strap around their shoulder. A new bus driver came on board once we were through the check point. Again, we had to list currency and show our passports. If they counted your money on return, and it was different than listed on one's entry, they would confiscate it. (The new guide's dialect was hard to understand.)

The Russian government paved a large wide street named Stalingradstrasse for show and propaganda. They pretended they were reconstructing the bombed-out buildings, but they remained in ruins. The streets in the distance had old, narrow buildings still showing signs of war. We were able to step out of the bus at the Soviet Memorial for the Russian Soldiers. This memorial was dedicated to all the Russian soldiers who were lost at the end of the war. Of course, the guard went overboard about Russia's involvement, giving statistics of their losses. But it was true; they lost a lot of servicemen.

I took special notice of one older lady dressed in dark clothing with a scarf over her head. She was down on her knees attending to a few flowers along the curb. She looked up from her gardening as the bus drove by. Her face was wrinkled and worn, which said it all to me. I wondered if she was an East Berliner forced to work for the Russians.

Val told me how her father's apartment house and beauty shop in East Berlin were seized. Her father was forced to reduce his staff and work longer hours. He no longer owned his own business or apartment house when the Russians took possession.

Val's parents were rationed as to how much coffee and food they could purchase. Her mother had to show worn-out shoes before new ones could be purchased. Val had the same shoe size as her mother. She bought new shoes and wore them across the border. When she returned to West Berlin, she wore her mother's old worn-out ones. Val hated the Russians who took over East Berlin where she was raised as a child. She wanted to get her parents released to the West. However, because they had owned an apartment house and ran the beauty shop of which the Russians took possession, they would not give her parents the necessary paperwork.

I saw a couple of old, broken-down, rusty-looking cars traveling slowly near the Brandenburg Gate. The East side looked so desolate. I was not in my comfort zone. The top of the Berlin Wall had sharp barbed wire and was backed up with tall buildings with windows cemented or bricked shut. When the wall first went up, people jumped from building windows adjacent to the wall to get to the West. The Russians now made it impossible to jump over the wall. Taking pictures was prohibited near the wall. The tour guide praised the main modern street which was empty except for tourists. We could take all the pictures we wanted there. The Russians wanted the West Berliners to think the East was prospering and modern—it wasn't! I was relieved once we were back safe in West Berlin.

West Berlin was such a contrast, bright and lively. The evening we returned, Fran and I went to a Hofbrau House, well known to be modern, with a band playing. Each table had linen tablecloths, a large number in the center and a modern white telephone handset. The numbers were visible throughout the circular-shaped room, including the balcony above. Men sitting at other tables sent a single red rose to the table where they wanted to request a dance. We received several roses, accompanied by the originating table number. We located the table number where the rose came from. In most cases we could see the gentlemen who was asking for the pleasure of a dance via telephone.

When a gentleman came to our table, Fran would talk in German or Dutch. We did agree to a dance a few times; it was fun and unique. Fran and I had a couple glasses of wine; she mostly did the talking over the telephone due to different languages. She was skilled—whether on the phone or face to face—with her interpreting. It was a fun and an exciting evening—great break from the day-to-day travel with Fran's mother and aunt. The club closed at four o'clock in the morning.

On Saturday, October 25th, a visit to the zoo proved worthwhile. Afterward, I drove the Opal around the city trying to trace the Berlin Wall. It went for miles around Berlin and irregularly divided the West from the East. We visited the Kaiser Wilhelm Memorial Church, which was bombed in WWII, but the original west tower remained. Afterwards, we headed back to Helmstadt.

About seventy-five kilometers away from the American sector, on the two-lane divided road, we were flagged down by Russians. Frightened, Fran asked in German what they wanted. They requested German currency in small denominations. Ruth and May had a lot of marks and gave them change for larger bills. The Russians seemed friendly enough. They claimed to Fran some Germans were caught speeding and smaller bills were needed to give them change after paying a large fine. It was a desolate part of that sector and scary. They left us go through after we exchanged money. When we got to the American sector we pulled over. I was shocked to see that even Ruth and May took a deep sigh of relief. I drove on to Helmstadt and we sought out a hotel to spend the night.

The next morning we headed back to Wiesbaden. I was driving at eighty-five km/h, and the car started misfiring. I pulled off the highway to a small-town garage. We stepped out of the car and the mechanic took the Opal for a test drive.

"It's *Kaput* and non-repairable," he said in broken English. There was dead silence among all of us.

"What do you want to do?" I asked, looking over at Ruth and May for a response. After all, this trip was for them, and they had been running the show. The original agreement was they would pay for the gas.

"We don't have a choice. Let's see if they will buy it from us," Ruth suggested.

May asked, "How do we continue our trip?"

Fran questioned the man about how much they would give us for the car.

"You need to pay fifty mark; we junk it," he remarked in broken English.

Fran spoke up: "Are you serious?"

I quickly responded out of desperation, "Let's try to go slow and see if we can make it to Hanover, a larger city." I thought to myself, *If we could just get back to Wiesbaden. It's time for me to return to the States.* I was tired of having to lug Ruth and May's baggage and adhere to their demands. I had been their servant long enough.

It was worth a try to baby the car forward. Otherwise, how would we all get back to Wiesbaden?

A consensus for a change was reached. We got back in the car and I drove slowly with it missing and knocking for miles. We made it into Hanover, and I pulled off the highway. I drove into a garage parking-place with the engine making a loud racket. The German spoke English and said it could be repaired. We were so happy to hear the news. It was hard to believe after being told it was *Kaput*. The Opal just had a burned-out valve, and we realized those former mechanics had lied to us. We left our car there for repair, and the mechanic drove us to a lovely Gasthaus for the night. He was to telephone us when the car was repaired.

We played cards all afternoon waiting for a call from the garage. It was six-thirty that evening when the car was ready. To our surprise, the repair bill came to only thirty-five dollars in American money. To think we would have given the car away and paid an additional fifty marks to those liars! Ruth and May were not overjoyed about the bill but didn't grumble. The repairmen were nice and threw in a rubber cover to better protect our suitcases on the roof. We had our Opal back, Ruth and May were back in the rear seat, me and Fran up front, and off we headed for Wiesbaden.

Going back and forth into hotel lobbies checking for hotel rooms in Wiesbaden for the relatives, I fell and hit my back against the curb and tore my slacks.

On Tuesday, October 27th, I was stiffened up after my fall but went to the post office for general mail delivery. The mail from Altoona and California was welcome news. But I received no letters from Paco, or his family. This was so disappointing after I had sent post-cards along my way. That evening, we met all the old gang at the Oberbryan. We sent Ruth and May back to their hotel by cab, and then we stayed until one o'clock in the morning. I threw up when Fran and I got back to the Eddies' flat; I'd had too much wine. One would think I would be conditioned by now.

I cleaned up the vomit in the sink and went back to bed with a hangover until two-thirty in the afternoon. I met Val for dinner and asked her to get us cans of motor oil for the car. It looked like Ruth and May wanted to continue the trip. I asked one of the airmen to buy me a sleeping bag. Fran and I could save money on the rest of the trip by sleeping in the car some nights. It was a long day with body aches and a bad headache. I got to bed at three-thirty that morning.

The next morning, I was still groggy from the hangover the day before. I drove to the police station to pay two parking tickets we had received. I talked the clerk into waiving one ticket; "I can't interpret German signs," I said, slightly raising my voice. I was telling the truth. I know the signs for the *Autobahn* or *Einbahnstrasse* (One Way) and *Verboten* (Do Not Enter), but not much more. Luckily for me, she waived the one ticket of five marks. Fran and I loaded the car and we headed for the Heidelberg Castle which was under reconstruction. It was one mark fifty *pfennigs* (pennies) to tour the castle and see the largest wine barrel in the world. Of course, we had a glass before finishing our tour. The castle was as cold inside as it was outside. It was a foggy day and hard to get any pictures.

I continued until Bobbingen outside of Stuttgart, Germany. Fran and I found a *gasthaus* for Ruth and May. We parked on a side dirt road, talked about our trip, and finally got situated in our sleeping bags about nine o'clock. The few cars that passed flashed their high beams at us; we ignored them. Suddenly there was a rap on our car window. I looked through the window and it was the Military Police. When I wound down the window a crack, he was surprised to see me, a woman, crawl partway out of a bag.

"Do you know who that car down the road belongs to?" He asked.

I answered, "No," rolled up the window, and got back into my bag.

Fran and I dragged out of our bags at seven o'clock the next morning, just as another MP came by. He asked to see our passports and said, "You two shouldn't be sleeping in the car."

I remarked, "It's better than driving into the night."

Fran smiled at me and explained, "You should have said, 'You are absolutely right officer.'"

I responded with a laugh. Fran was right; I should not have argued with the police. We picked up Ruth and May and arrived in Munchen at three o'clock that afternoon. We drove to the military base and an airman, Bill, escorted us onto base to the snack bar. We told him we were going to visit the Hofbrau Haus later. Bill said, "I'll see you there."

The Hofbrau was like a big barn with accordion music, everyone singing and prosting beer or champagne. We drank large steins of beer that you needed both hands to lift to your mouth. German waitresses with large bosoms, in typical short Bavarian outfits, carried those huge steins around. Bill showed up and we sat together on wooden benches listening to music until the band quit playing.

Afterward, we went to a rustic place down the street. The highchairs were hard to climb onto. We sat at small tables by the dance floor. Fran and I danced with Bill. He offered to take us sightseeing the next afternoon. We walked around the October Fest grounds until four o'clock in the morning.

Ruth awakened Fran and me at eleven that morning. "It's time to leave here," she ordered. I had to jot Bill a note of regret and drop it at the front desk. Fran and I had little say in the matter when Ruth made up her mind. Fran and I packed up the car as usual—which we were getting a bit tired of. Ruth expressed her desire to visit the Dachau Concentration Camp where all the Jews were exterminated. So, off we went to Dachau to see the depressing crematoriums and life-like pictures of prisoners before their death. Pictures of the liberation showed those emaciated Jews who survived starvation and cruelty welcoming the American soldiers. It ruined my day thinking of all that happened here. I was glad to get in the car and drive toward Vienna.

We stopped for dinner at a Gasthaus about 150 kilometers from Vienna, Austria. It was bright and cheery. The guests were friendly and introduced themselves. We were asked about Goldwater and President Johnson. They had heard Goldwater said all Austrians were Communists. We laughed and told them that wasn't true. This was a welcomed relief after Dachau. Ruth wanted to push onward to Vienna. We arrived at twelve o'clock midnight.

I was driving through center city when the gear shift located on the steering wheel column suddenly broke off into my hand as I shifted into second gear. I looked over at Fran in the passenger seat and she busted out laughing. It was funny, all right. But it was only seconds later that reality sank in. I was lucky it broke in second gear so I could keep driving. It took us an hour driving around in second gear to find a hotel after midnight. Ruth and May were not happy campers, finding out about another breakdown. And the question was, could it be fixed right away? I was beat and went to bed amid their complaining.

It was late the next morning when I started driving the car—still stuck in second gear—looking for a repair shop. An Opalhaus agreed to fix the gear shift while we toured the city. We visited the Parliament, Rathaus, and various monuments. Unfortunately, the opera was sold out. Fran and I checked on ski resorts hoping we would get a day at a ski resort soon. The nearest snow was 120 kilometers away.

The next day we went to the American Express office so I could file a claim for lost Traveler's checks. I filled out forms; the paperwork had to go to New York first before reimbursement. My hope was that my calculation was correct in losing three checks. If I received a refund, I would have more cash. I bought some small German Stein mugs for my cousins and miniature wooden skis with poles that hold toothpicks or matches as souvenirs. I purchased tickets for the Volksopera for all of us. The opera was great with music from Ravel. The sets were the best I've seen in some time. The first act was in French and the second in German.

That day was Election Day in the United States; we would know the results the next day. We drove back through a part of Germany to get on track toward Innsbruck. We stopped near the city at another Gasthaus. The small houses in the Bavarian villages were picturesque, painted in bright colors like a fantasy land. Fran and I were looking forward to reaching a ski area soon.

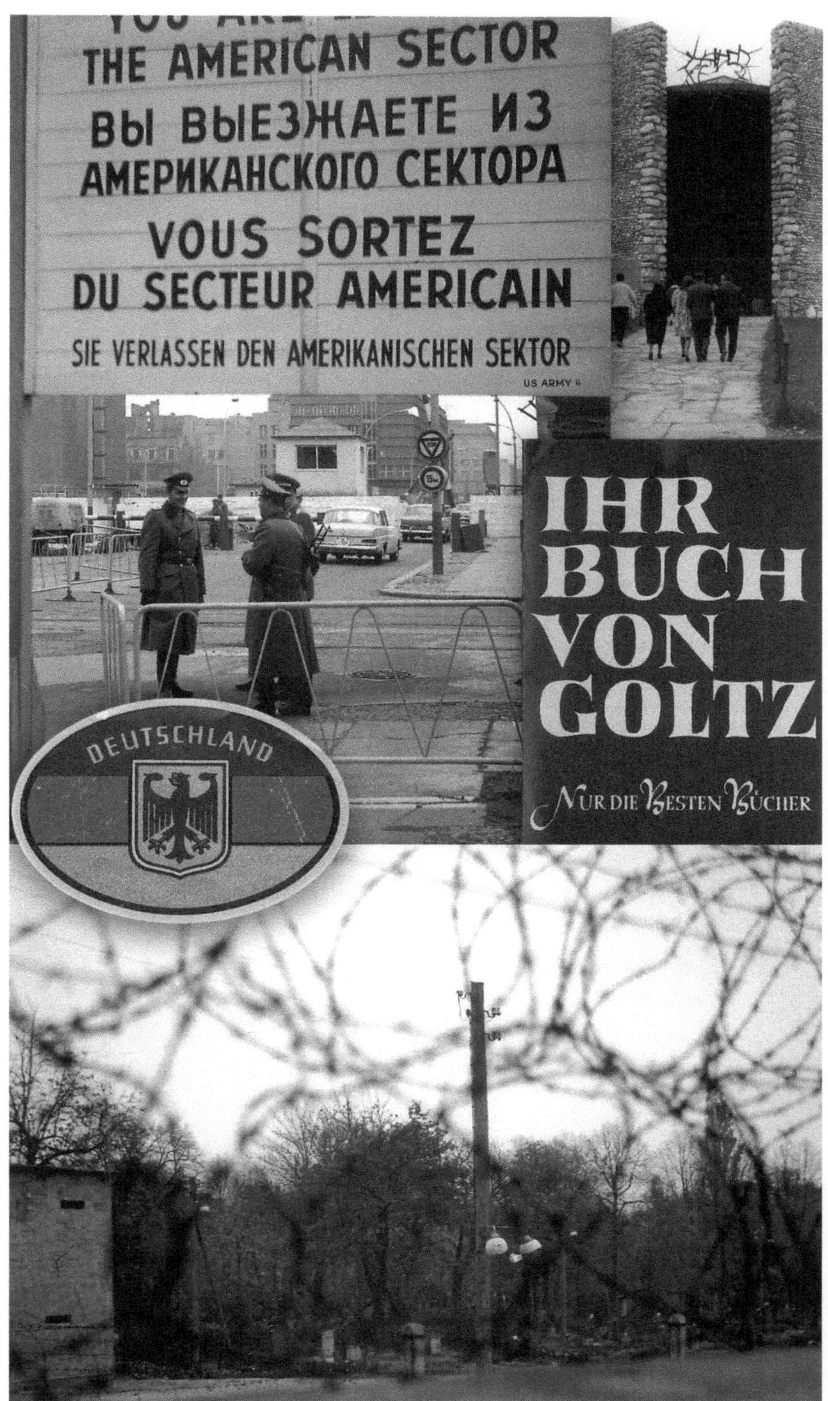
THE AMERICAN SECTOR
ВЫ ВЫЕЗЖАЕТЕ ИЗ
АМЕРИКАНСКОГО СЕКТОРА
VOUS SORTEZ
DU SECTEUR AMERICAIN
SIE VERLASSEN DEN AMERIKANISCHEN SEKTOR
US ARMY
IHR
BUCH
VON
GOLTZ
NUR DIE BESTEN BÜCHER
DEUTSCHLAND

U S ARMY
CHECKPOINT CHARLIE
Gösser-Bier
Budapest
Klagenfurt
Südautobahn

Welcome to
BERLIN
BERLITZ
GERMAN
FOR TRAVELERS
PHRASE BOOK And
Glossary of Common Words
WHAT TO SAY:
When you arrive
In restaurants
At your hotel
„Vier Jahreszeiten"
HOTEL - RESTAURANT
1000 BERLIN 31 (WILMERSDORF)
Bundesallee 31 a
Ruf 87 20 14
Datum 23.10.64
Rechnung
Übernachtung 21.10. / 23.10.64 54,–
Frühstück 12,95
„Vier Jahreszeiten"
HOTEL - RESTAURANT
1000 BERLIN 31 (WILMERSDORF)
Bundesallee 31 a
Ruf 87 20 14
Datum 24.10.64
Rechnung
Übernachtung 23.10. / 24.10.64 20,–
Frühstück 9,35
über den Kurfürstendamm
MIT LUFTPOST
PAR AVION
LESS, BARNEY +
ANNA LOWBERGER
2652 NEWELL ST.
LOS ANGELES 39
CALIFORNIA
U.S.A

Speisegaststätte, Fremdenzimmer
„Zum Auerstein"
Inh. Martin Hebner
69 Heidelberg
Dossenheimer Landstraße 82
Telefon 06221/40798

RECHNUNG Datum 21.4.73

für Fa./Herrn Zimmer-Nr. 1

	Einzelzimmer		
1	Doppelzimmer	32	–
1	Bad	2	50
	Speisen u. Getränke		
	Telefon		
	Sa.	34	50

Betrag dankend erhalten:
„Zum Auerstein"

In diesem Betrag sind Bedienung und 11 % Mehrwertsteuer enthalten

Auf Wiedersehen! Gute Fahrt!

GASTHAUS ZUM „Salmen" RASTATT (BADEN)
BESITZER WILHELM KÜHN
Am Grün 26, an der Ankerbrücke · Telefon 2355
Gut bürgerliche Gaststätte · Sämtliche Zimmer mit fließendem kalten und warmen Wasser · Zentralheizungen · Garagen

RECHNUNG Datum 28. 7. 1964

für Herrn Zimmer Nr.

Zimmer	7.	–
Frühstück	2.	80
Speisen		
Getränke		
	9.	80
Bedienung	–	90
Garage	2.	–
Telefon		
Heizung		
DM	12.	70

Betrag dankend erhalten:
Kühn

Ich wünsche Ihnen eine gute Weiterreise!

ESSO

…UNG

	DM	Pf.
…EXTRA	5,	60
DIESEL		
MIX	0	55
…XTRA MOTOR OIL		
…-T MOTOR OIL . .		
…MOTOR OIL . . .		
…UB MOTOR OIL . .		
	3,	–
Gesamtbetrag	9	15

…nd erhalten

28. Juli 1964

Tag

A 58 11. 63

Gasthaus z. alten Post
Hôtel Pension
INH. B. SEMADENI · Ø 081/8 62 35
ZILLIS

Rechnung für Hr. J. L. Foor
Note pour

angekommen den / arrivé le 29. 7. 64 Zimmer / Chambre No. 8

	Ganze Pension / Arrangement		
1	Zimmer / Appartement	5.	50
1	Morgenessen / Petit Déjeuner	2.	70
	Mittagessen / Lunch		
	Nachtessen / Dîner		
		8	20
	15% Service	1	25
	1 x Taxe	–	20
		9	65

FRANKFURT AM MAIN
Hauptwache, Dom, Eschenheimer Turm
Hauptbahnhof

17.

Hi Janie –
What's wrong? I haven't gotten any mail from home for so long. I guess everyone is pretty busy or they don't care to write to me anylonger. I'm in Frankfurt now & should start working soon with one of two places – Amer Express or Intl Tel & Tel Co. Both good jobs. Lots of men around & I'm having a great time. Will be living with an Amer girl & her father in their apt. next week.
Pls write! c/o Amer Express
NEUE MAINZER STRASSE 25
FRANKFURT am MAIN, GERMANY
Love – Jenis

LUFTPOST

MISS JOAN FOOR
2654 NEWELL ST
LOS ANGELES
CALIFORNIA
USA

Viel Freude am Fahren!

LE

Couvert	
1 chambre No 8	10.00
1 Repas	9.50
1/2 Roche	2.20
1 garage	1.00
Montant	22.70
Service 15 %	3.40
Total	26.10

…ble No

07

Grüße aus FRANKFURT am Main

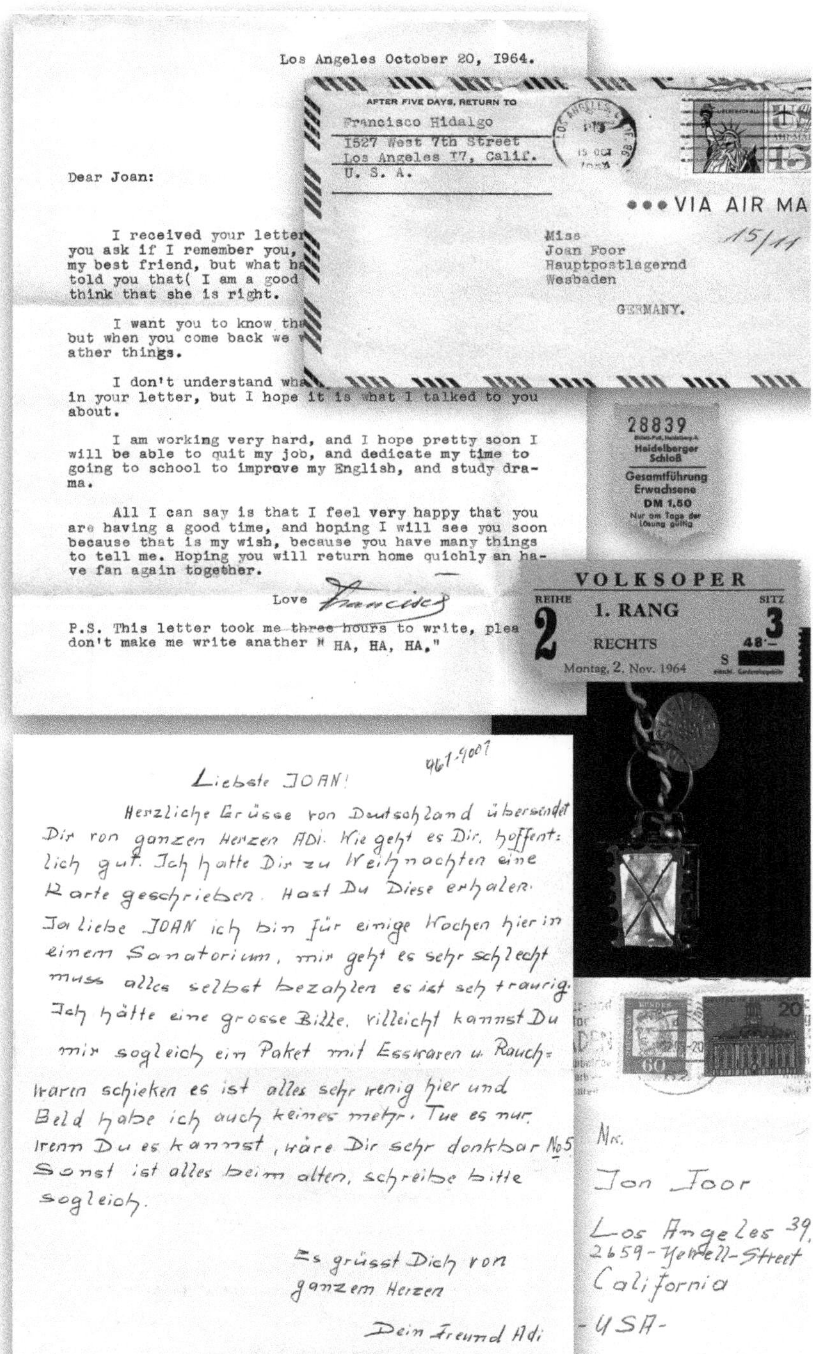

Los Angeles October 20, 1964.

Dear Joan:

I received your letter ... you ask if I remember you, ... my best friend, but what ha... told you that(I am a good ... think that she is right.

I want you to know th... but when you come back we ... ather things.

I don't understand wha... in your letter, but I hope it is what I talked to you about.

I am working very hard, and I hope pretty soon I will be able to quit my job, and dedicate my time to going to school to improve my English, and study drama.

All I can say is that I feel very happy that you are having a good time, and hoping I will see you soon because that is my wish, because you have many things to tell me. Hoping you will return home quichly an have fan again together.

Love Francisco

P.S. This letter took me three hours to write, plea... don't make me write anather " HA, HA, HA."

AFTER FIVE DAYS, RETURN TO
Francisco Hidalgo
1527 West 7th Street
Los Angeles 17, Calif.
U. S. A.

VIA AIR MA...

15/11

Miss
Joan Foor
Hauptpostlagernd
Wesbaden
GERMANY.

28839
Heidelberger Schloß
Gesamtführung Erwachsene
DM 1,50
Nur am Tage der Lösung gültig

VOLKSOPER
REIHE 2
1. RANG
RECHTS
SITZ 3
48.–
S
Montag, 2. Nov. 1964

961-9007

Liebste JOAN!

Herzliche Grüsse von Deutschland übersendet Dir von ganzen Herzen ADi. Wie geht es Dir, hoffentlich gut. Ich hatte Dir zu Weihnachten eine Karte geschrieben. Hast Du Diese erhalen. Ja liebe JOAN ich bin für einige Wochen hier in einem Sanatorium, mir geht es sehr schlecht muss alles selbst bezahlen es ist seh traurig. Ich hätte eine grosse Bitte, villeicht kannst Du mir sogleich ein Paket mit Esswaren u. Rauchwaren schicken es ist alles sehr wenig hier und Geld habe ich auch keines mehr. Tue es nur wenn Du es kannst, wäre Dir sehr dankbar No5 Sonst ist alles beim alten, schreibe bitte sogleich.

Es grüsst Dich von ganzem Herzen

Dein Freund Adi

Mr.
Jon Foor
Los Angeles 39,
2659-Yewell-Street
California
-USA-

ERNST HEINKEL AKTIENGESELLSCHAFT
STUTTGART-ZUFFENHAUSEN
POSTFACH 76

Ernst Heinkel AG. Kundendienst
6 Frankfurt/M. Kleyerstr.42-44

Miss
Joan L. F O O R

L.

IHRE ZEICHEN

BETREFF: He

Se

Na
Si
sc
Be
na
na
Wi
Be
ab

Mi

Er
6

i.

Banken: Württ.

Allg. 055b GI

ERNST HEINKEL AKTIENGESELLSCHA
STUTTGART-ZUFFENHAUSEN

By Air Mail

Miss Joan L. Foor
2654 Newell Street

Los Angeles 39 Calif.

USA

Ernst Heinkel
6000 Frankfur
Kleyerstrasse

7 Stuttgart-Zuffenh
Hellmuth-Hirth-Straße
Postfach 76
Telephone Collective

Dear Miss Foor,

Thank you for your letter dated February 26. We woul
to excuse us for not having written to you earlier.
letter has been lost and we did not know your addres

Your scooter is still unsold, but, together with the
people have now appeared who may be interested in buy
ever they will not be prepared to pay more than 600,
Please be kind enough as to let us know by return of
we are to sell it at this price or whether we shall
until you will return for another trip in Europe.

Looking forward to your reply we remain

Yours sincerely,
ERNST HEINKEL KUNDENDIENS

Du: Kundendien

DEUTSCHE BUNDESBAHN

TOURISTISCHE STRASSENVERKEHRSDIENSTE DER EUROPÄISCHEN EISENBAHNEN

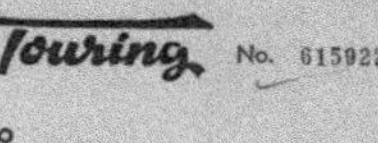

No. 615922 *

DEUTSCHES REISEBÜRO

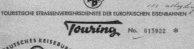

Los Angeles October 20, 1964.

Dear Joan:

I received your lette
you ask if I remember you,
my best friend, but what ha
told you that(I am a good
think that she is right.

I want you to know th
but when you come back we
ather things.

I don't understand wha
in your letter, but I hope it is what I talked to you
about.

I am working very hard, and I hope pretty soon I will be able to quit my job, and dedicate my time to going to school to improve my English, and study drama.

All I can say is that I feel very happy that you are having a good time, and hoping I will see you soon because that is my wish, because you have many things to tell me. Hoping you will return home quichly an have fan again together.

Love Francisco

P.S. This letter took me three hours to write, plea
don't make me write anather " HA, HA, HA."

AFTER FIVE DAYS, RETURN TO
Francisco Hidalgo
1527 West 7th Street
Los Angeles 17, Calif.
U. S. A.

••• VIA AIR MA

15/11

Miss
Joan Foor
Hauptpostlagernd
Wesbaden

GERMANY.

28839
Heidelberger Schloß
Gesamtführung
Erwachsene
DM 1,50
Nur am Tage der Lösung gültig

VOLKSOPER
REIHE 2
1. RANG
RECHTS
SITZ 3
48.–
S
Montag, 2. Nov. 1964

967-9007

Liebste JOAN!

Herzliche Grüsse von Deutschland übersendet Dir von ganzen Herzen ADI. Wie geht es Dir, hoffentlich gut. Ich hatte Dir zu Weihnachten eine Karte geschrieben. Hast Du Diese erhalen. Ja liebe JOAN ich bin für einige Wochen hier in einem Sanatorium, mir geht es sehr schlecht muss alles selbst bezahlen es ist seh traurig. Ich hätte eine grosse Bitte, villeicht kannst Du mir sogleich ein Paket mit Esswaren u. Rauchwaren schieken es ist alles sehr wenig hier und Geld habe ich auch keines mehr. Tue es nur, wenn Du es kannst, wäre Dir sehr dankbar No5 Sonst ist alles beim alten, schreibe bitte sogleich.

Es grüsst Dich von
ganzem Herzen

Dein Freund Adi

Mr.
Jon Foor
Los Angeles 39,
2659 - Yewell - Street
California
- USA -

ERNST HEINKEL AKTIENGESELLSCHAFT
STUTTGART-ZUFFENHAUSEN
POSTFACH 76

Ernst Heinkel AG. Kundendienst
6 Frankfurt/M. Kleyerstr.42-44

Miss
Joan L. F O O R

L.

IHRE ZEICHEN

BETREFF: He

Se

Na
Si
sc
Be
na
na
Wi
Be
ab

Mi

Er
6

i.

Banken: Württ.

Allg. 055 b 03

ERNST HEINKEL AKTIENGESELLSCHA

STUTTGART-ZUFFENHAUSEN

By Air Mail

Miss Joan L. Foor
2654 Newell Street

Los Angeles 39 Calif.

USA

Ernst Heinkel
6000 Frankfur
Kleyerstrasse

7 Stuttgart-Zuffenh
Hellmuth-Hirth-Straße
Postfach 76
Telephone Collective

Dear Miss Foor,

Thank you for your letter dated February 26. We woul
to excuse us for not having written to you earlier.
letter has been lost and we did not know your addres

Your scooter is still unsold, but, together with the
people have now appeared who may be interested in buy
ever they will not be prepared to pay more than 600,
Please be kind enough as to let us know by return of
we are to sell it at this price or whether we shall
until you will return for another trip in Europe.

Looking forward to your reply we remain

Yours sincerely,
ERNST HEINKEL KUNDENDIENS

Du: Kundendien

DEUTSCHE BUNDESBAHN

TOURISTISCHE STRASSENVERKEHRSDIENSTE DER EUROPÄISCHEN EISENBAHNEN

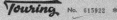

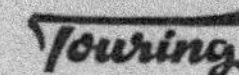

No. 613922 *

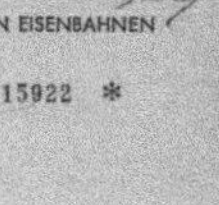

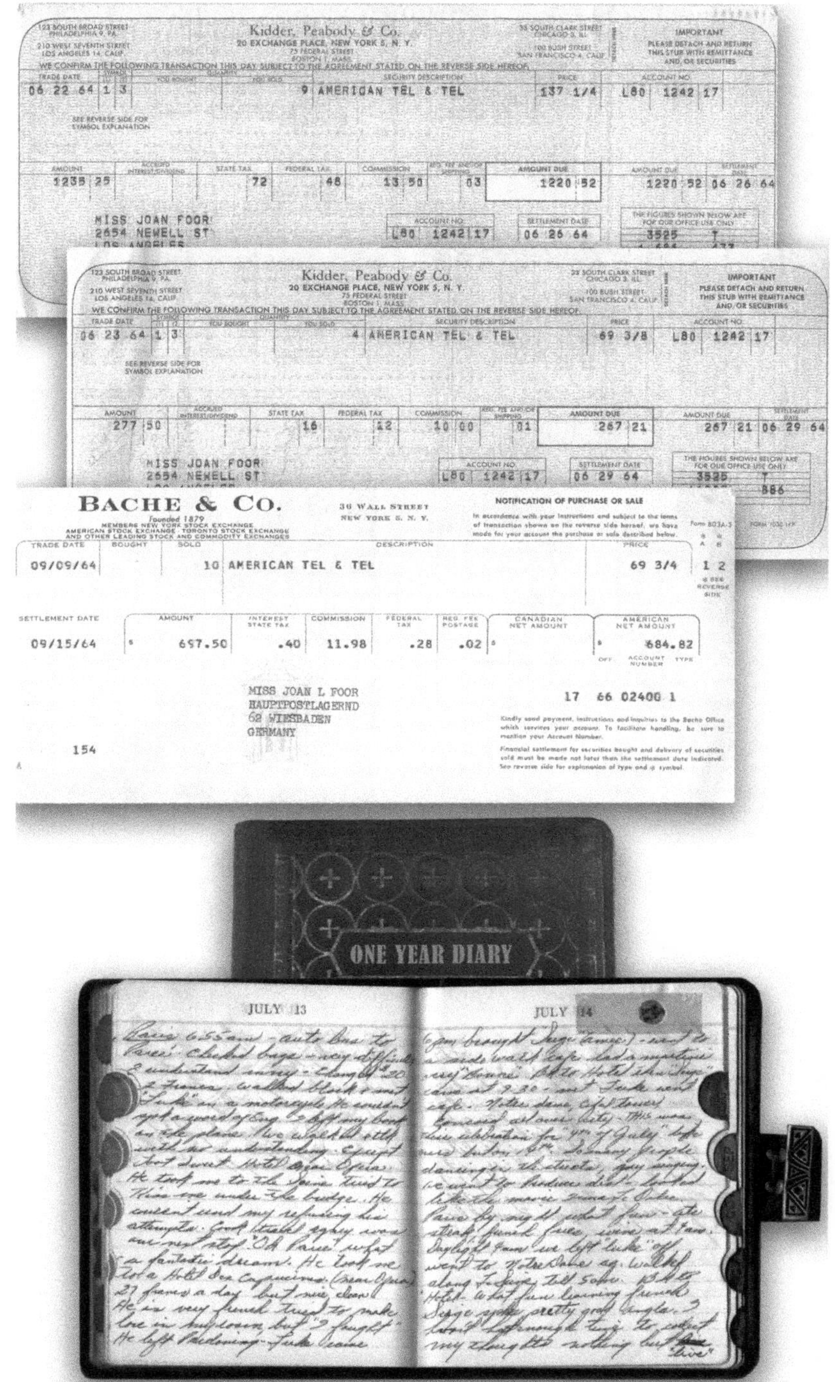

Kidder, Peabody & Co.
20 EXCHANGE PLACE, NEW YORK 5, N. Y.
75 FEDERAL STREET, BOSTON 1, MASS.
123 SOUTH BROAD STREET, PHILADELPHIA 9, PA.
210 WEST SEVENTH STREET, LOS ANGELES 14, CALIF.
35 SOUTH CLARK STREET, CHICAGO 3, ILL.
100 BUSH STREET, SAN FRANCISCO 4, CALIF.

IMPORTANT: PLEASE DETACH AND RETURN THIS STUB WITH REMITTANCE AND/OR SECURITIES

WE CONFIRM THE FOLLOWING TRANSACTION THIS DAY SUBJECT TO THE AGREEMENT STATED ON THE REVERSE SIDE HEREOF.

TRADE DATE	SYMBOL		YOU BOUGHT	YOU SOLD	SECURITY DESCRIPTION	PRICE	ACCOUNT NO.
06 22 64	1	3		9	AMERICAN TEL & TEL	137 1/4	L80 1242 17

SEE REVERSE SIDE FOR SYMBOL EXPLANATION

AMOUNT	ACCRUED INTEREST/DIVIDEND	STATE TAX	FEDERAL TAX	COMMISSION	REG. FEE AND/OR SHIPPING	AMOUNT DUE	AMOUNT DUE	SETTLEMENT DATE
1235 25		72	46	13 50	03	1220 52	1220 52	06 26 64

MISS JOAN FOOR
2654 NEWELL ST
LOS ANGELES

ACCOUNT NO. L80 1242 17 — SETTLEMENT DATE 06 26 64 — THE FIGURES SHOWN BELOW ARE FOR OUR OFFICE USE ONLY: 3525 T

Kidder, Peabody & Co.
20 EXCHANGE PLACE, NEW YORK 5, N. Y.
75 FEDERAL STREET, BOSTON 1, MASS.
123 SOUTH BROAD STREET, PHILADELPHIA 9, PA.
210 WEST SEVENTH STREET, LOS ANGELES 14, CALIF.
35 SOUTH CLARK STREET, CHICAGO 3, ILL.
100 BUSH STREET, SAN FRANCISCO 4, CALIF.

IMPORTANT: PLEASE DETACH AND RETURN THIS STUB WITH REMITTANCE AND/OR SECURITIES

WE CONFIRM THE FOLLOWING TRANSACTION THIS DAY SUBJECT TO THE AGREEMENT STATED ON THE REVERSE SIDE HEREOF.

TRADE DATE	SYMBOL		YOU BOUGHT	YOU SOLD	SECURITY DESCRIPTION	PRICE	ACCOUNT NO.
06 23 64	1	3		4	AMERICAN TEL & TEL	69 3/8	L80 1242 17

SEE REVERSE SIDE FOR SYMBOL EXPLANATION

AMOUNT	ACCRUED INTEREST/DIVIDEND	STATE TAX	FEDERAL TAX	COMMISSION	REG. FEE AND/OR SHIPPING	AMOUNT DUE	AMOUNT DUE	SETTLEMENT DATE
277 50		16	12	10 00	01	267 21	267 21	06 29 64

MISS JOAN FOOR
2654 NEWELL ST

ACCOUNT NO. L80 1242 17 — SETTLEMENT DATE 06 29 64 — THE FIGURES SHOWN BELOW ARE FOR OUR OFFICE USE ONLY: 3525 T 886

BACHE & CO.
Founded 1879
MEMBERS NEW YORK STOCK EXCHANGE, AMERICAN STOCK EXCHANGE, TORONTO STOCK EXCHANGE AND OTHER LEADING STOCK AND COMMODITY EXCHANGES
36 WALL STREET, NEW YORK 5, N. Y.

NOTIFICATION OF PURCHASE OR SALE

In accordance with your instructions and subject to the terms of transaction shown on the reverse side hereof, we have made for your account the purchase or sale described below.

TRADE DATE	BOUGHT	SOLD	DESCRIPTION	PRICE	A	B
09/09/64		10	AMERICAN TEL & TEL	69 3/4	1	2

SETTLEMENT DATE	AMOUNT	INTEREST STATE TAX	COMMISSION	FEDERAL TAX	REG. FEE POSTAGE	CANADIAN NET AMOUNT	AMERICAN NET AMOUNT
09/15/64	$ 697.50	.40	11.98	.28	.02	$	$ 684.82

MISS JOAN L FOOR
HAUPTPOSTLAGERND
62 WIESBADEN
GERMANY

17 66 02400 1

154

Kindly send payment, instructions and inquiries to the Bache Office which services your account. To facilitate handling, be sure to mention your Account Number.

Financial settlement for securities bought and delivery of securities sold must be made not later than the settlement date indicated. See reverse side for explanation of type and @ symbol.

Telegramm
Deutsche Bundespost
GNC2516/CD= LLC236 ANGLES CALIF 12/11 6 1001
JOAN FOOR HAUPTPOSTLAGERND
WEISBADEN =
TSt Wiesbaden
D 93 C NY WUN USA
DAD DIED THURSDAY HOME= AUNT ANNJ+U
WARNING
IMPORTANT:
JOAN LOUISE FOOR
MARCH 21, 19
PENNSYLVANIA, U.S.A.
BLOND
BROWN
X X X
X X X
PASSPORT RENEWAL
PHOTOGRAPH ATTACHED
DEPARTMENT OF STATE
LOS ANGELES
IMM. & NATZ. SERVICE
NEW YORK, N.Y. 39
ADMITTED
NOV 13 1964
CLASS
Visas
SVERIGE
14 OKT 1964
DDR
Udrejst den
24 OKT 1964
10
11
Kodak
BRIGHT SUN
HAZY SUN
SHADE
2.8
Brownie
8 MM. MOVIE
CAMERA II
13 MM f/1.9 LENS
Visas
P.I.D.E.-PORTUGAL
23 AGO 1964
ENTRADA
31 AGO 1964
SAIDA
POLICIA
SALIDA
Indrejst den
8
9

Chapter Fifteen: Innsbruck

On Wednesday, November 4th, we arrived in Innsbruck, and the Austrian Alps in the background were covered with snow. We ran into a fellow who stated that his brother was on the Ski Olympic Team. He directed us to Zurs Ski Resort in Austria where an early powder lay.

Ruth and May insisted we drive them to Garmisch on the border of Southern Germany first. We arrived there and walked around to satisfy Ruth and May. We then headed for Zurs.

The noise in the rear end of the car was beginning to worry me, especially when I drove in low gear.

Zurs did have about a foot of fresh powder. It was beautiful, and the roads were plowed. I stopped to have antifreeze put in the radiator. Fran looked over and smiled, realizing we were finally going to go skiing. We stopped at a resort hotel, and the ski lift was operating. Some hotels were not open for the season yet. Fran and I had our plan to get into the city and rent skis early.

It was half past six the next morning when we went to the car. It was covered with a light snow. We were delighted with being surrounded by a winter wonderland. I tried to fire up the engine. All I got was a click; the battery was dead.

Fran was determined; "Let's go to the main road and hitch a ride." I followed her out to the small road. A Singer sewing machine van came by and gave us a lift. We rented skis, boots and hitched another ride back to our hotel. The temperature had warmed up some, and the car started. We loaded up our ski equipment and drove to the nearest chairlift. Finally, we had some fun.

Fran wasn't that agile on skis. When she fell, I had to help her up. I laughed as she tried to use her poles to stand up. After over three hours we knew Ruth and May would be getting restless.

"Joan, we had better get back, or mother will have a fit," Fran said.

"Fran, let's take one more run. It's already too late to drive farther today. Besides, it will freeze over, and our tires are bald."

I hopped onto the chair lift and up I went. Coming down the hill, I suddenly confronted a narrow creek in my path. I had no choice but to jump over it—and I made it! I didn't know when I had ever had so much fun. We met up with some Japanese skiers practicing for the future Olympics and a few Americans waiting for the lift.

Fran's mother was fuming when we got back. She got Fran so upset, she began to stutter. I decided to step in: "Ruth, it will be dark soon. We can't take off now. It isn't safe to drive with those smooth tires in the ice and snow."

She glared at me and replied, "You and Fran planned this and knew what you were doing."

I walked away from her. I thought, *This time she's right; we did trick her and May somewhat. But it was more than well deserved.*

The next morning Ruth said, "We want to see Italy. It isn't far according to our map."

"Mom, this is winter, and we will have to go through mountains. I think we are asking for trouble." Fran glanced at me as she spoke.

"Well, we've come this far, and your aunt and I want to see Italy," she declared with both hands on her hips.

"I'm not sure the car will make it; but if that's what you want, I'll try to get you there," I replied, but not without concern.

I drove us back through Switzerland. Suddenly the back, passenger-side tire blew out. I pulled to the side of the road. I checked the trunk and we didn't have the proper tools to fix it. In addition, it was dark out. A young man stopped along the road to help us. He changed the tire and I paid him with a couple packs of American cigarettes. I continued to Buchs, Switzerland, on the border of Liechtenstein, where we stopped for the night.

The following morning I went out to buy a used tire just in case we had another blow out. After I loaded the spare tire in place, we set out for Italy. I had to drive in low gear through the Jullier Pass in the Alps; the elevation and switchbacks were causing the rear-end noise to worsen.

We were near Lake Como and drove on to Lugano at the northern border of Italy. The drive made me a nervous wreck. But we got to eat Spaghetti in Chiavenna, Italy, a magical little town. Most of all, Ruth was able to say she had been to Italy. I gulped down two glasses of wine, which enabled me to drive farther around the twists and turns of the narrow road with ease.

On Saturday, November 7th, we drove back to Switzerland and had breakfast.

"I can't find my traveler's checks!" May yelled at us frantically, as she rooted through her purse after eating. She most likely had lost them last night in Italy. There was no way we were going to backtrack trying to find them. I drove ahead through the Alps' Siplon Pass. It was dangerous, for patches of ice still covered the road, having not melted, and small drifts of snow were everywhere.

We made it to just outside Lausanne, Switzerland. Fran and I were looking forward to the next day. It was back to Paris for me. Ruth and May would head back to the States. May planned to pick up her money for lost travelers checks in Paris. It looked like the ol' Opal might make it after all.

We had about 150 kilometers to touchdown. I drove the car up over a curb under a streetlamp so I could see to add a quart of oil. About fifty kilometers later, a loud bang came from beneath the car. I pulled to the side of the road and crawled partway under the left side. The main spring had broken and was dragging on the road. We were in luck. I saw an Opalhaus farther down the road. I drove slowly into a hotel with the spring dragging on the street.

The next morning I drove the Opal to the Opalhaus at eight

o'clock. They replaced the spring, but it wasn't finished until noon. I paid for it and headed back to the hotel.

"You broke the spring, and you should pay for it," Ruth scolded. May nodded her head in agreement as our eyes met.

"Okay, Joan and I will pay for it," Fran spoke up, disgusted. Later, I didn't tell them how much it really cost. I had paid for it myself because I knew Fran had little money. It was twenty-eight American dollars—I would let May and Ruth think they got away with not paying a much larger bill. I drove like mad, without stopping, straight into Paris.

We arrived at three-thirty that afternoon, just in time to get May to the American Express office. I whipped around my old hangouts: the Champs-Élysées near the Opera House, and the old hotel where I had stayed months before. I took them to the large department store, Galeries Lafayette. I bought some small vials of perfume in little, blue-velvet, drawstring bags for all my aunts back home. Ruth and May finally got to see a department store that I believed surpassed even Macy's in New York. It was an eye opener for any tourist who went there.

It was time to drop Ruth and May off at the Gare du Nord. We said our goodbyes.

"Fran, we will see you back home soon," Ruth went on. Fran looked sad as she hugged Ruth and May goodbye. I delivered a cheek-to-cheek hug after helping with the luggage.

"Have a safe trip; it's been quite a journey," I said, meaning every word.

Fran's plan was to pack all her things and move back to Brooklyn when we got back to Wiesbaden. Fran had planned to show them Europe when they retired, and she had done it! Fran and I walked back to the car, not looking back. When we got inside the car, we both took a deep breath.

"I met my promise and did my best to satisfy them," Fran said, rather sadly.

"C'mon, Fran, you went overboard. Those two aren't the best of travelers. I don't care if it is your mother or not; she can be almost impossible at times. Believe me, I was ready to throw in the towel several times but couldn't. You know none of you were able to drive along the way."

"Thanks for sticking with me. At least we had several hours of skiing," Fran added. We both busted out laughing at the same time. We were off to our destination; Wiesbaden, once again. We drove until three o'clock in the morning and stopped at a Rastplatz. We crawled into our sleeping bags for the last time.

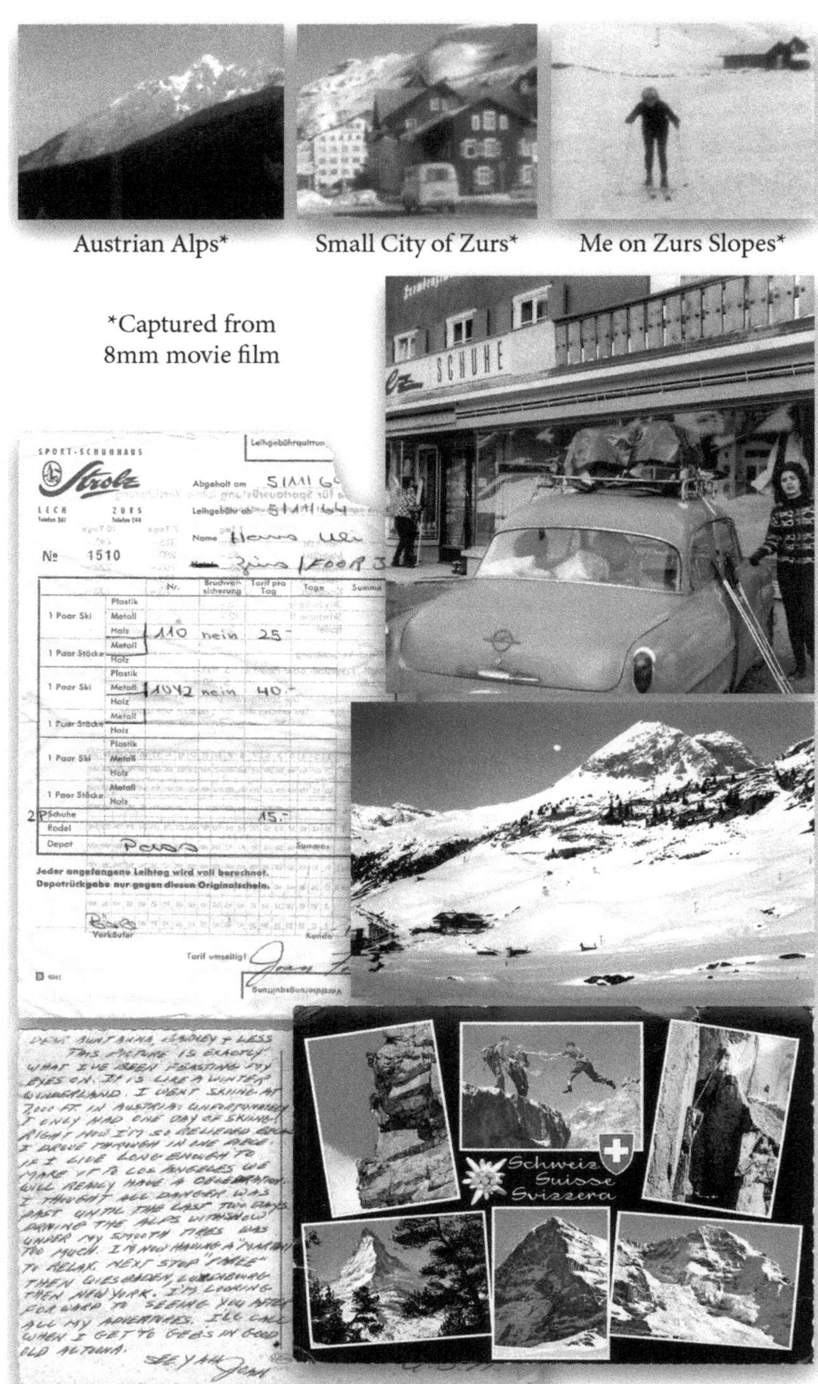

Austrian Alps* Small City of Zurs* Me on Zurs Slopes*

*Captured from 8mm movie film

DEAR AUNT ANNA, SADLEY + LESS
THIS PICTURE IS EXACTLY WHAT I'VE BEEN FEASTING MY EYES ON. IT IS LIKE A WINTER WONDERLAND. I WENT SKIING AT 7000 FT. IN AUSTRIA. UNFORTUNATELY I ONLY HAD ONE DAY OF SKIING. RIGHT NOW I'M SO RELIEVED I DROVE THROUGH IN ONE PIECE. IF I LIVE LONG ENOUGH TO MAKE IT TO LOS ANGELES WE WILL REALLY HAVE A CELEBRATION. I THOUGHT ALL DANGER WAS PAST UNTIL THE LAST TWO DAYS. DRIVING THE ALPS WITH SNOW UNDER MY SMOOTH TIRES WAS TOO MUCH. I'M NOW HAVING A "MARTINI" TO RELAX. NEXT STOP "PAREE" THEN WIESBADEN, LUXEMBOURG THEN NEW YORK. I'M LOOKING FORWARD TO SEEING YOU AFTER ALL MY ADVENTURES. I'LL CALL WHEN I GET TO GEB'S IN GOOD OLD ALTOONA.
SEE YAH
Joan

Chapter Sixteen: Return to Wiesbaden

We arrived back in Wiesbaden at noon after driving about five hours. I drove immediately to the post office to check for mail. A telegram was waiting for me. It read: "Dad Died Thursday Home—Aunt Ann."

I sat down on the bench with a sadness overcoming me. To think I'd been looking at souvenirs for Dad the entire trip. I wondered did he get my last postcard, stating that I would be coming home in a couple of weeks.

"What's wrong, Joan?" Fran came over to where I was sitting. I handed her the telegram.

After reading, Fran said, "I'm so sorry. What are you going to do?"

"Where can I find a pay telephone to call Pennsylvania?" I asked.

"Come with me. I'll take you to one." We hugged and Fran took me by the hand, leading me down the street to a red phone booth near the Bahnhof. I telephoned Aunt Beb's house and reached my brother Les. I didn't know where to begin, "Les, I'm so sorry. I can't believe Dad is gone."

"Joan, we buried Dad this morning. I held up the funeral for a week hoping to hear from you," Les explained.

"Les, I was traveling and didn't get the telegram until this afternoon when I returned from Paris. My plan was to return home in the next few days. A couple of days ago, I mailed a card to Dad saying I would be home soon. If I had sent it sooner, perhaps he would have hung on, knowing I was on my way home. We will never know. He was holding his own when I saw him in early July. I never dreamed Dad's condition was that bad, or I would have come home sooner."

"Sis, I understand, but I have some trouble. Maggie, his mistress, will not leave Dad's house. She is making a claim that the house is hers now. After all, she has lived with Dad as a common law wife and a caregiver for several years."

"What? You mean to tell me she is still at the house and making a claim to it?"

"Yes, and she is hanging on. I can't find any Last Will and Testament. A lot of Dad's papers are strewn all over the cellar floor. I've been sorting through it, but it's mostly bills." Les continued.

"Well, you tell that woman if she is not out of the house by the time I arrive, I will throw her out physically. I'm getting the first plane I can afford out of here. How are you holding up after all this?" I asked him.

"I'm doing okay. It's been hard at the funeral home and putting Dad to rest. I do need to get back to my job. I'm catching a plane back to L.A. in a couple of hours. Get home safely, Sis. I'll see you back in California. We have a lot of catching up to do."

"Thanks for taking care of everything. I'm so sorry I wasn't there. I'll telephone when I get back to the states. Bye for now." Tears began to flow down my cheeks as I hung up. I wished Les could have stayed there until I got back. I looked at myself in the mirror. My hair roots had grown out on the trip about an inch, and I generally looked unkempt. I spent the day reminiscing about Dad and Mother. I hadn't been able to say a final goodbye to either, and I was full of regret. I went to bed at Grandma's. She awakened me at 12:30 a. m.

"We heard about you father's passing. Get out of bed. Ed and I are taking you for a drink," Edith said, pulling at my arm. They took me to some of our old hangouts. But it wasn't the same tonight. I couldn't get Dad and his mistress out of my mind. The club we were at closed, so they took me back to Edith's flat. She threw sleeping bags on the floor and I crawled in. I tossed back and forth for hours before falling off to sleep.

Ed shook my arm at ten o'clock in the morning. "We need to pick up Val at the Frankfurt airport. She is coming back from visiting her parents in Berlin. Hurry up and come with us," he said. I splashed some water on my face, changed into slacks, and tried to pull myself together.

The first words out of Val's mouth were, "I'm going to fly back to New York with Fran. I've talked to Alan again, and I'm going to join him as planned in the States. Joan, you can join Fran and me. We'll all go together."

That sounded good. I left Val and Ed and went shopping for cheeses and souvenirs for everyone back home. After I returned to Edith's, we had a drink and proceeded to the Oberbryan. After that, we stopped at the Park Café and closed the place down.

It was back to Edith's afterwards. Several cups of coffee, which I rarely drink, didn't help much to sober me. I hit the couch at four o'clock that morning and was wide awake. I mulled over missing my Dad's funeral. I got up, still wasted and light-headed, at seven that morning I pulled out my suitcases and started packing for home.

Fran came rolling in at ten o'clock in the morning, announcing, "I'm not going stateside. I cancelled my reservations."

"Fran, are you serious?" I asked. "What about your mother and Aunt May, who are expecting you?" I asked.

"I can't face going back to live with Mother after all these years. You know what she's like. I just can't do it!" Fran explained.

Fran had been out all night with her boyfriend. I'm sure he had given her reassurance to stay where she was the happiest. I met Val later and we went together to buy our bus and plane tickets. We would travel by bus to Luxembourg, where we would board Icelandic Airlines.

"Do you think Fran is doing the right thing by staying in Germany?" I asked. "It sounds as though she can't bear the thought of living with her mother again. After all, she's been here in Europe for years. She lived in Holland and now Germany for the past several years."

"After I saw how the two interacted on our trip, I'm not surprised. Her mother makes her nervous, and she begins to stutter. I don't think she's strong enough to stand up to that woman. I personally had enough of Ruth's domineering ways on our trip. I feel sorry for Fran. She's insecure when it comes to her mother," I explained.

We drove to the Bahnhof a few blocks from there and weighed our bags. My head was still pounding, and Val didn't feel that great either when we returned to Edith's.

"Fran, I'll leave the Opal at the Bahnhof and hide the keys under the front mat. You can pick our little ol' car up later," I instructed. "I'm off to the States and I'm sorry you are not going with us. But I do understand. We had quite a trip together. You kept your promise to your mother and aunt. We saw to it, didn't we? I wish you the best of luck! Take care, my friend."

Our teary eyes met. We had been through quite an ordeal together. We hugged goodbye. I joined Val at the curb. I drove me and Val to the parking zone near the Bahnhof. We walked to the bus area inside. I looked back over my shoulder at the old Opal. I smiled to myself. The old car had gotten me through the worst weather. It was sad leaving the car behind. This would be the last leg of my journey. We were off to Luxembourg; after that it would be Iceland and then America.

Val and I slept most of the flight. It didn't matter that we were stuck in the economy section. I hadn't slept for three days; I was still hungover, as was Val. Our stop in Iceland was less than an hour. We crossed the windy tarmac just to grab a bite to eat. Val was excited to meet her old boyfriend, Al, in New York. She'd lived with him while he was stationed in Germany for about a year. He was transferred back to the States and promised to marry Val if she came back to the U.S.

As for me, I had been away from Paco long enough to realize how much I really missed him. I had met a lot of interesting men along the way. Some had potential but I never gave any of them a serious thought. No men I met even halfway stirred up the feelings I had for Paco. The excitement of the trip kept me from feeling lonely, nor did I have time to dwell on our physical separation. This was especially true because I was visiting his family and felt secure about our relationship. My journey was to put our love to the test and explore the possibility of a future with Paco in Spain or who knows.

Chapter Seventeen: New York and Pennsylvania

Going through customs in New York was the worst. The customs agent questioned Val and rummaged through her suitcases. "Miss Brooks," he asked, "you mean to say you are claiming nothing when you have resided in Germany for the past several years? What about all of this lingerie?" They continued to thumb through the rest of her clothing in her suitcases.

"Officer, I've worn all you see here. I've bought nothing new," she remarked. Her voice in broken English was sounding so innocent and sweet. She stood there before them in a mink, three-quarter-length coat. I looked over at her and had to contain myself from busting out laughing.

When they got to me, it was a disaster. They opened my bag with all the bratwurst, cheese, and chocolate bars. Into the trash went all the cheese and meat. I was furious. I was able to keep the candy bars. I did have a few trinkets of souvenirs, but it was all under one hundred dollars.

"I've nothing to claim," I uttered forth, arrogant and disgusted.

It was a long line to have our passports checked. The customs agent said, "Welcome back to United States, Miss Foor." That was the only positive statement I had heard in the last few hours. On the other side of the glass partitioned area was Al with a big grin on his face.

I immediately thought about Paco. I wondered why I hadn't heard from him in months. I did hear from his sister in Barcelona, who stated they were so glad to have met me. However, I had no mail from Paco, nor did Pilar mention anything about her brother.

"You look beautiful," Al said lifting Val off her feet and kissing her passionately. At that moment I was jealous, wishing the same thing was happening to me; I could imagine the feeling of Paco lifting me up and saying how much he had missed me. Val looked back at me, and we started laughing because we looked as though we had been on a binge for days!

Val introduced me to Al, and we made our way through the crowd. Al had his car parked near the airport and I headed for the train station. It was time to say goodbye after the long flight back to New York. We hugged, then I said, "I'll telephone when I get to Pennsylvania. What a trip, Val!"

I picked up my suitcases and walked away. Al took Val's bags and off they went. My ankles were sorely swollen, making it an uncomfortable walk to the bus area. I picked up a cab from where the bus dropped me off near Penn Central Station. I purchased a PRR train ticket to Altoona, Pennsylvania.

During the hour and one half waiting for my train, the noise was next to unbearable. They were drilling and blasting in Penn Central Station; I guess it was a remodel. In the interim, I tried to exchange some German money—no luck. They wouldn't exchange coins. I dropped some Denmark coins in the public telephone. To my surprise, they registered like American dimes. I talked with Fran's mother, Ruth, and told her Fran decided to stay in Germany. She was shocked and disappointed. After getting to know Ruth, I believed Fran had made the right decision to be happy.

I telephoned Paco collect in Los Angeles, saying, "I'm in New York and on my way to Pennsylvania. However, my Dad passed away, so I need to spend some time at my home in Altoona." I waited for a response.

"Joan, I'm sorry for the loss of your father. Do whatever you have to do. You've been gone a long time. We've a lot to discuss," he added.

"Yes, it has been a while," I replied. "It was great meeting your family. They are wonderful, kind people. I've been carrying a new pair of shoes from your sister Pilar all over Europe. I took movies of everyone and will get them developed when I get back to show you."

"That's great, Joan. Please come home," Paco insisted. After hanging up, I thought, *He didn't say I missed you, but then again neither did I. He was right; it had been a long time—almost five months.* I rooted through my coin collection and found more Danish "ore." The telephone accepted more of these coins as I telephoned Aunt Beb in Pennsylvania. After she answered, I said, "Aunt Beb, I'm coming by train and will arrive in Altoona at seven in the evening. Can you pick me up?"

"You bet," she answered quickly. "Thank heavens you're safe! We have been worried since we couldn't reach you about your Dad. Maggie is causing problems and your brother is too soft with her. That woman threw herself into your Dad's casket, making a fool out of herself at the funeral home. She's nothing but trouble. Get yourself home here. I'll be at the railroad station waiting."

"Thanks, I can't wait to deal with that woman," I said angrily. "And believe me; I will not be easy on her. See you soon, Aunt Beb."

I hung up with thoughts of how Maggie tore our family apart. Les and I had discovered she had slowly poisoned our mother to keep her weak and bedfast for a year. This was because she was having an affair with our dad. She wanted to continue to live in our house as a caregiver. She denied giving Mother the wrong medication when we confronted her. Mother ended up hospitalized leaving the way clear for Maggie to remain as Dad's live-in mistress. This was my opportunity to tell her exactly how I felt out in the open. I no longer had to go easy to protect Dad's feelings or the care he received from her.

I met a Frenchman on the train, which helped pass the time. I enlightened him about my travel to Paris and other highlights along my journey. I noticed passengers across the aisle listening to our conversations. Had it not been for him welcoming me back home, I was ready to hop a plane and return to Spain.

New York was being such a disappointment. I had lost all

the different cheeses I wanted to share with relatives. And today was a letdown after five months of excitement. Everything had come to a quick halt when I found out about the loss of my father. Although I was planning to return to the States once I got Fran and her family back to Germany; Dad's death was a shock and hastened my trip home.

Aunt Beb picked me up at the train station as planned. She filled me in on the way to her house about what had transpired during and after the funeral.

"You have got to deal with Maggie and get her out of your dad's house," she said.

"My plan is to go down there tomorrow," I told her. "I will take Uncle Glen and Aunt Shirley with me because I told them on the phone that I will let them have Dad's refrigerator. I felt bad when I visited them before leaving on my trip. The door hanging from their refrigerator was tied shut with a rope. Here I was, going to spend money on a trip when they needed help. Dad's refrigerator is only a few years old. It's the least I can do, and Dad would be pleased I could put it to good use." I said.

"You needn't feel guilty about spending money you earned and saved," Aunt Beb replied.

Aunt Shirley and Uncle Glen met me in front of Dad's house the next morning. I was prepared to let Maggie have it with all the stored-up anger and dislike I had held for her for years. I ran up the porch steps and barged into the house with Uncle Glen right behind me.

"Maggie, where are you?" I rushed through the living room, into the dining room and kitchen. She was not there. I went to the stairwell, "Get down here before I come up and drag you down!" I yelled. There was no response.

I went up the stairs with Uncle Glen right behind me. I checked all the rooms. She was gone. I looked in the clothes closets and just Dad's clothes remained. It was a bit of a disappointment, for I was unable to release all those pent-up emotions. My blood pressure must have been terribly high. I walked down the stairs to the kitchen. I began to calm down and helped Uncle

Glen move the refrigerator away from the wall. He used a dolly to load it onto his truck.

Maggie never showed up at the house again. I had no idea where she had gone, nor did I care. It took me two weeks to settle what I could about Dad's estate. Les had already contacted an attorney, "It will take about a year to settle everything, since you could find no will." He advised.

"I was approached by our neighbors, the Hetrick's, who are interested in buying the cottage at Long Bend. Please give them consideration if the price is right for them. I gave them your name to contact later," I said.

I met Beverly, Joyce, Helen, Kathy, and Mary Jo at Olivio's to say goodbye. Joyce Walker dropped in later and we closed the place. It was fun, all of us old co-workers from Bell Telephone together again.

Les telephoned the next morning, "Joan, what's going on? Why haven't you called?"

"I've been busy visiting everyone. I went down to the cottage and brought Dad's fishing box up to pack. I gave the boat to Aunt Beb and Uncle Pete. Also, I'm going to pack up Dad's favorite guns and ship them out," I went on.

"You haven't mentioned Maggie. What happened with you and her?

"I was ready to let her have it, and I took Uncle Glen as backup. I ran all through the house like a tornado. She was nowhere to be found. I checked and even her clothes were gone. Good riddance. But I was sorry I couldn't tell her off like I wanted to for years."

"Well, Joan, it's for the best. She might have thrown something at you or hurt you in some way. I'm glad she was gone," Les said.

"I will telephone Aunt Anna and give her my flight number. I'm going to pick up an airline ticket tomorrow for the day after Thanksgiving. I want to spend Thanksgiving Day with the relatives."

"I'm glad. Tell everyone "Happy Thanksgiving" and get yourself home, Sis."

"Les, wish everyone out there the same," I said.

Aunt Beb and I baked six pies and went to Aunt Shirley's and assisted with stuffing the turkey. It was a great old-fashioned Thanksgiving. I telephoned Aunt Anna and told her my flight number and arrival time for the next day. Afterward, Beverly came, and we took a pie to Kathy's house. Mary Jo and Helen were there.

The next morning Aunt Beb drove me to the Martinsburg Airport. Cousin Karyn rode along. Janet Keim, another previous co-worker and her husband met me at the airport for a short visit before boarding. We were remembering old times and laughing when I heard, "Stop the plane; my niece hasn't boarded," Aunt Beb yelled running along the window inside the terminal. I rushed to the window and saw my twin engine plane on the runway turning around getting ready for takeoff.

"Never mind, Aunt Beb. It's too late! Janet, her husband and people in the terminal looked over at us. We couldn't believe I missed my plane to Pittsburgh. I checked at the ticket counter and the next flight was for the same time the following day. Well, we had a nice visit at least. Aunt Beb drove me back to the Automobile Club to change my ticket for the next day. I telephoned Aunt Anna and told her what happened, and I would be coming home one day later.

We left at the same time the next morning for Martinsburg. About halfway there, the fan belt broke in Aunt Beb's Corvair car. Luckily, she had an extra one and we replaced it. Corvairs were notorious for breaking fan belts. I made it to the airport just in time to board the plane for Pittsburgh with a transfer to Los Angeles. It was a thrill to fly the small puddle-jumper, looking down at the Pennsylvania farmland and rolling hills to Pittsburgh.

Once aboard my plane for L.A., I had six hours to think about where I had been and what I had experienced. In my mind all the questions I had were answered. I had no doubt that I'd remained true to Paco. I understood his temperament after meeting his family and traveling through Spain. The separation proved my love for him was strong and I could hardly wait to see him and share the news.

ALTOONA, PA., WEDNESDAY, NOV

ONE WAY TO SEE EUROPE—Joan Foor, daughter of the late Mr. and Mrs. Russell L. Foor of Altoona, is shown on her Heinkle motor scooter in Weisbaden, Germany, before she began her 10,000-mile trip which took her as far as Tangiers in North Africa, by way of Gibraltar, for about two months this summer. She wanted to see the area her brother, Leslie, now of Los Angeles, was stationed in while he was in the service.

FINDS TRIP INTERESTING

Altoona Girl Back From European Scooter Tour

She traveled alone across Europe and into North Africa on a Heinkle motor scooter this summer and with a girl friend by an Opel car into Scandanavia this fall, but the highlight of four months vagabonding for Miss Joan Foor, 28, former Altoonan, was nearly drowning in the Atlantic surf at a Lisbon beach in Portugal on Aug. 30.

Miss Foor, who is staying at the home of Mrs. Genevieve M. Soyster of 1807 6th St. until she returns Friday to her job as a receptionist with the Pacific Telephone Company at its Hollywood, Calif., office, said of her trip, "I loved it. I may go again."

"In this materialistic world, I was trying to get away from it all," Miss Foor said in explaining her primary reason for making the trip. "I would never be content to live in the hardship people do over there, but just going made me more relaxed.

"I wanted to go backward in time, live in the old days and do the hard things they had to do," she said. "But hot water and a comfortable bed are very good."

She confessed that one of her purposes was to visit the mother in Barcelona, Spain, of a friend in California. He is Frank Martin, who before he came to the United States two years ago was Francisco Hidalgo.

Visiting with Senora Hidalgo for a week was quite an accomplishment, since Miss Foor had only one year of high school Spanish (she graduated from Altoona High in 1954) and the Hidalgo family possessed no English. Sign language and gestures can be eloquent, Miss Foor learned.

But for her travels—she emphasizes she desired to see average people and live under average conditions—she equipped herself with Spanish, French, Italian and German dictionaries. And she did well, too, thank you.

Arriving in Paris July 12 by Air France, she went to Weisbaden, Germany, where she bought her Heinkle for 800 marks, about $206. She'd never ridden a motor scooter before, but set off by herself for her trip to Tangiers, to see the area where her brother, Leslie, had been stationed.

She went south to Rome through Switzerland on her scooter stopping at modest hotels and pensions. In Italy, she found quarters outside of Rome in a old fortress-type accommodation on a hilltop at Frascotti, from which she sallied forth to see the area.

Then she swung into the Iberian peninsula by way of the Cote D'Azur, stopped at the Hidalgo home in Barcelona, and by way of Gibraltar, got to Morocco and Algeria. It was on her return through Lisbon she almost finished her trip.

Swimming in the Atlantic, she found the undertow too strong to get back to shore. She battled the water for an hour, vainly trying to attract attention. Just as the lifeguards saw her she was slammed up against a reef, from which she was rescued by Portuguese lifeguards. They formed sort of a human chain to get her off the reef, since they had no boat.

Refusing to let a bruised body and scratched legs deter her, she set off on her Heinkle for Paris and returned to Weisbaden. The Heinkle now is up for sale in a shop there and she'll get the money when it is sold.

But a girl friend of hers from Brooklyn, whom she knew in Weisbaden, talked her into buying an Opel, for which they paid about $200. In it, the girls set off in late September for Belguim and Holland. Then they went to Copenhagen and Oslo and ended up returning through West Germany into East Berlin. Joan even got in some skiing at Zurs, Austria, before the trip was over. The Opel added 7,500 miles to the 10,000 miles she covered on the Heinkle.

The Opel is now up for sale at Weisbaden in the custody of her friend from Brooklyn, who at the last moment decided not to return to the States.

It was a trip Miss Foor had been "planning" for a couple of years. But when the big moment came, it happened suddenly. She was enroute back from the World's Fair when she decided to ask for a six-month leave of absence. She flew to Europe without knowing whether her request had been granted. She learned it had sometime later.

Her expenses for the four months, she estimates, were about $1,500, exclusive of the vehicles, on which she hopes to get a return.

"It's not cheap to live in Europe," Miss Foor said. "In Spanish hotels, you can get a good average room for from $1.50 to $2 a night. I stayed in one for 42 cents, but don't recommend it. In northern Europe and the Scandanavian countries, at moderate hotels used by the natives, it costs from $2 to $4 per night."

"Everyone is friendly," Miss Foor reported. "Everywhere I was treated well. You could get a job there, but you can't save money."

But living on the same scale as the natives, traveling off the beaten paths and staying at non-tourist facilities, she discovered, gives you an insight into the country which the average tourist never gets. "And there's a lot of Europe I haven't yet seen," she said.

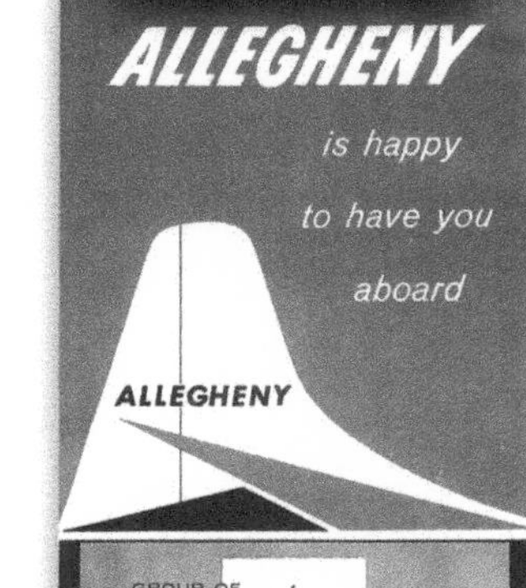

assenger ticket and baggage

LOFTLEIDIR
ICELANDIC AIRLINES

YOUR BAGGAGE IS CHECKED TO
NEW YORK
LOFTLEIDIR
3-17-73
3-17-76

Chapter Eighteen: Los Angeles and Home

The moment I arrived back inside my little tenant house behind Aunt Anna's main house, I telephoned Paco.

"Paco, I'm back home in L.A.," I announced. "I'm here to stay, and I'm anxious to see you. How are you? It took longer than I expected to get things straightened out back there since my father's death."

"It's fine," Paco replied. "I'm sorry about your father. You were gone a long time, Joan. Things have happened. I told you not to go. Why didn't you listen?" He paused.

"What are you saying, Paco? Are you all right? You sound worried and anxious."

"I'm okay. We have a lot to discuss, Joan."

"I have much to share with you about your wonderful family. As I mentioned from New York, your sister Pilar sent you a pair of new shoes from her store. Your mother sent embroidered handkerchiefs and socks. I've brought them here for you," I said.

"I want to see you, Joan. I'll come right over."

"Paco, I want you to know I don't have the pictures or movies of your family yet. It will take about a week from now to have them developed. I'm anxious for you to see them." I went on.

"Never mind about that, Joan. I should be there in about twenty minutes," he said anxiously.

"I'll be waiting."

I put down the phone. It was about thirty minutes later when I heard a rap at my front door. I rushed to greet him. There stood the love of my life on my front steps. He had on white tennis shorts, a white open collar shirt. Paco had a great tan as usual and his brown curly hair was still bleached from the sun. He looked fantastic and fit as always.

I opened the door wider, and he rushed in like a tornado giving me a hurried kiss on the cheek. He continued into the living room and flopped down on the couch.

"I can't stay. I have an appointment, but things have changed, Joan," he avoided looking straight at me. I felt empty inside and sensed something was terribly wrong, but what?

"What's going on? You sound so out of breath and anxious." I picked up his new shoes and things from his mother and laid them on the couch beside him. He barely glanced at them and continued to look downward toward the floor.

"Remember, Joan, I told you not to go. Well, things have happened. You were gone a very long time. And, well, I met this woman. She's very wealthy and lives in the Hollywood Hills."

I stood motionless and stunned when I asked, "Well, what about her?" Obviously, there was more to come.

"I've never seen anyone with so much wealth. She is helping me with my playwriting. You knew when you left that I was working on my screenplay," he continued.

"So, that's it!" My heart began to pound faster. I could feel throbbing up the sides of my neck. I was speechless, not knowing what to say next. I had just gone around the world to meet his family. I was in disbelief of what was happening here. My lips were quivering when I asked, "How serious is this?"

"I don't know. I'm not sure yet." He kept shifting positions on the couch and fidgeting about. I walked over taking hold of his chin, raising his head up so our eyes could finally meet.

"Have you fallen in love with her?" I asked, looking straight into his eyes.

"Remember, I begged you not to go without me. But you insisted and would not listen," he scolded. He made it sound as though I had turned my back on him. I had never lost sight of my reasons for going. He was pressuring me. I had needed time away from him to ensure this was true love. It was a test. Meeting his family and visiting his country were an important part of it.

"I'm sorry, Joan, but I've got to go now. I wish I had more time, but I don't." He pushed my hand away, got up and headed for the front door.

"Paco, wait!" I grabbed hold of his arm. He was resisting. "Please don't go, Paco! We need to talk this over. So, this is my fault. Is that what you're saying? How could you let this happen? There I was, visiting your family and getting their acceptance into the family, and you were running around? What kind of a man are you?"

"Joan, I'm sorry I've upset you, but I've got to go!" He pulled away from my grasp.

"For God's sake, go on then!" I was devastated. He opened the door and went rushing down the driveway. I stood at the doorway watching the man I loved hurry away from me, not knowing what to think. I had traveled around the world to make sense of my love for him, and now this? I flopped down on the couch and bawled out loud. It was like a nightmare. I don't know how long I sobbed, thinking about what had just taken place. Finally, I freshened up in the bathroom and pulled myself together.

I fired up my old Volkswagen parked in the back of the driveway. Aunt Anna or Les must have started it while I was gone. I dropped all the films at Savon's Store to be developed. I returned home and waited by the phone. I thought he might call with a further explanation. He did not.

I lay awake my eyes wide open. I turned every which way begging for sleep, but my mind kept going over what had happened. I thought, *He never really said he loved me. I remember him telling me I was beautiful, but not once could I remember him, in so many words, say he loved me. But then again, did I openly say I loved him?* We were in love at the time, but obviously it wasn't strong enough on his part. Was it really my fault for leaving? Perhaps it was. However, the desire for him along with pressure from work led me to believe I had to get away from it all. I visited his family, learned more about his customs and country. The trip was to find out if I could marry him with his temperament. After five months of separation, meeting his family, and traveling about Spain, I believed Paco was the man for me. Did I have a chance now to compete with this rich woman—I came back from Europe with only a hundred dollars in my pocket.

The next morning, out of desperation, I telephoned Paco. I needed to calm down and get clarification on exactly where our relationship stood. I was surprised to hear a female voice on the other end of the line. Thinking it probably was his housekeeper, I asked, "When do you expect Paco?"

"I'm not sure. This is his wife speaking. Did you wish to leave a message?"

I dropped the phone! So *that* was it! I flopped down on the couch and then hung up the phone. Tears rolled down my cheeks. He didn't have the guts to tell me the truth. No wonder he was in such a hurry to leave—he could barely face me!

To think this entire trip was mostly because of him. Was I naïve to think he would be waiting for me? I certainly never seriously considered any of the men I met on my journey. Oh, there were plenty of flirtations, but I stopped them in their tracks. I was always faithful to Paco. I never doubted his love for me.

I don't know how long I sat there stunned. It was time to cry out to someone. I walked next door to see Aunt Anna and told her what had happened. She was furious and said, "I'm so sorry, honey. I know you were in love with him. But I must admit, your brother and I had our doubts about this relationship. I didn't want to hurt you, but I never felt he was the right man for you. Don't be so hard on yourself."

"But, Aunt Anna, should I have known better than to think he would join up with me or be patiently waiting for my return? I had no reason to doubt his sincerity, especially since I was visiting his family. They accepted me without question as though I was to be the new daughter-in-law."

"European men think and act differently honey. I know how hard it is for you now; but give yourself time. Think about what you have seen and experienced these past months. You are still young and somewhere out there is a man who will be right for you. I'm sure of it!"

Epilogue

Here it is decades since I made what I consider to be the trip of my lifetime. I often wondered what happened to Paco, our paths never crossed again. The six months leave of absence I requested turned out to be granted for only three. I lost my seniority of ten years with the telephone company. They agreed to hire me back but with my brother, Les's, encouragement I left their employment. I drifted between several jobs for almost three years. I tried selling advertising, displaying greeting cards in department stores, and even did a short stint in a Gershwin Broadway show as a dancer in Hollywood.

In 1967, I enlisted in the U.S. Army to serve my country during the Viet Nam War. My desire was to become a helicopter pilot only to find out they did not train women pilots in 1967. My second choice was in their nursing program. My exposure taking care of the sick and wounded began my career into this field. After over three years of active duty I sought a Bachelor's Degree in Nursing at Mt. St. Mary's College in Los Angeles while continuing to serve in the U.S. Army Reserves.

I married a wonderful man who had many of my same interests. We had a successful marriage enjoying hunting, fishing and traveling. My husband liked to take off on his Harley motorcycle, but I could not relax riding as a double. He purchased a 500 Honda for me to ride alongside. Due to the busy roads in California I was not comfortable out on the open road like before. Riding through Europe in 1964 was peaceful. We took to traveling by a camper instead. He passed away at the young age of fifty-seven.

My brother, mother, aunts and uncles have since all left this world. They were all wonderful mentors. I acquired a position as an assistant administrator in a busy rural Kaiser Permanente Medical Clinic. The clinic was located in Lancaster California. Later, I took the position as the administrator. I continued my education and was granted a Master's degree at UCLA in Ambulatory Care and Pediatrics as Nurse Practitioner.

For twenty-six years I traveled to USC Medical Center in Los Angeles one weekend a month. I was in charge of nursing training for enlisted soldiers and junior officers through the U.S. Army Reserve Nurse Corps. I retired from Kaiser Permanente after thirty-eight years of service and retired from the U. S. Army Reserves as Lieutenant Colonel after twenty-nine years.

After retirement, I worked as an adjunct professor for the BSN program at the University of California, Bakersfield and several years at Antelope Valley College's two-year Nursing Program.

I consider myself totally retired now, at eighty-four. (Although I continue to advise friends and relatives concerning their health and medical care.) I divide my time between keeping-up a summer home in Palmdale Hills, California and a winter residence near Palm Springs, California. My desire to travel remains. In the U.S. I drive my small Rialta recreational vehicle along with my best friend Pam; my dog, Daisy, and cat Monkey. My visits abroad have been to many new places: Alaska, Australia, Canada, England, Indonesia, Egypt, Israel, Jordan, Nova Scotia and Russia. I continue to get a kick out of returning to many of the countries and cities I saw for the first time over fifty years ago.

Things may have changed these past fifty years, but the fond memories of my trip of a lifetime endure in my heart.